By My Own Rules

By My Own Rules
MA ANAND
SHEELA

MY STORY IN MY OWN WORDS

EBURY
PRESS

An imprint of Penguin Random House

EBURY PRESS

USA | Canada | UK | Ireland | Australia
New Zealand | India | South Africa | China

Ebury Press is part of the Penguin Random House group of companies
whose addresses can be found at global.penguinrandomhouse.com

Published by Penguin Random House India Pvt. Ltd.
4th Floor, Capital Tower 1, MG Road,
Gurugram 122 002, Haryana, India

First published in Ebury Press by Penguin Random House India 2021

Copyright © Sheela Birnstiel 2021

10 9 8 7 6 5 4 3 2 1

ISBN 9780670094523

Typeset in Minion Pro by Manipal Technologies Limited, Manipal
Printed at Replika Press Pvt. Ltd, India

www.penguin.co.in

*I dedicate this book to everyone who
has helped me through my life*

Contents

Author's Note

By My Own Rules is a collection of glimpses from my past. At the age of 71, I see it as an opportunity to remember those adventurous and intense moments.

It is my mother, father and Bhagwan that I have learned from in my life. This trio has prepared me to accept life as it comes. They have developed in me the concept of being there and living in the moment. They have given me the understanding to complete the circle of my life by my own rules.

Although the book covers a lot about my profession, I have also spoken about my experiences and feelings.

Over the last three decades, I have taught myself the ropes of my profession. I've learned on the job, worked closely with the residents with diverse conditions including dementia. The different systems, themes and dealing from my work in this book are 100 per cent my experiences and observations.

These are no pre-learned theories. They are all real-life situations.

For this treasure trove of learning, I am grateful to my residents. Their trust in me reminded me that simply being there for them was the ultimate solution.

Foreword

When it comes to writing the foreword for a book by someone I consider the true heiress of Osho, the responsibility is greater than one imagined. After all, it's not only about the content of the book but also about the unique person behind the story, about what makes her so special, and about the message she carries to the world.

Sheela was born as Ambalal Patel Sheela in Baroda, India. In the 1980s, she was a faithful companion of the world-famous Bhagwan Rajneesh, also known as Osho. She founded and led the Rajneeshpuram Commune in the USA. Despite the difficult times Sheela experienced as a consequence of her leaving Bhagwan Rajneesh, she continues to be loyal. Her love for her former teacher and master continues to be boundless. I have not come across another person with as much capacity to love. In her book *Don't Kill Him!*, which provides an insight into the whole story, she also describes how she got to know and love Osho. She describes herself as a lover of Bhagwan.

Today, after all the trials and tribulations of her life, she has created her own paradise in Switzerland, where she runs two homes for the old and the ailing whom she cares for. Sheela gives them immeasurable love and comfort because that is what these people need. Love and care. She has developed the invaluable concept of 'being there' which addresses the two aspects that most care-homes suffer from, isolation and abandonment. At the end of the day, all of us want to be loved and cared for. In this she has been a role model for many people, giving them hope and confidence.

Sheela is one of the most influential spiritual mentors of the twenty-first century even though she has never called herself a spiritual teacher, master or guru. She is love on all levels of her being, a living example of pure loyalty and lived spirituality. No one has touched and impressed me as much as she has.

Her life illustrates that the answer to the questions many people are looking for is always love. That's what Sheela is all about. That's what makes her special. She doesn't judge people. She has never held anyone responsible for what happened to her, and has always taken responsibility for her own decisions. She has demonstrated that no matter what happens on the outside, she will continue to follow her heart. Her deep conviction for what she believes in determines her actions. As this book details, it was pure gut feeling, innate intuition that led her to leave the one person she loved, and continues to love, unconditionally. In doing so, this book shows how important it is to just turn off the mind and trust your inner voice because everything you feel is true; it is your own truth.

Sheela is not only a friend and companion for me. She is much more than that; she is part of my family. I would like to end by saying, 'Glow and shine not only like a star, but like an entire universe.' It fills me with the greatest pride to be able to write the foreword to her book, *By My Own Rules*. I hope readers across the world read the book, and find out the true story of Sheela.

Your Saint von Lux
Rorschacherberg, Switzerland

Rule 1

Pain cannot be avoided; pain has to be endured

There are certain moments—demanding, trying—that define our approach to life. They become the reference points for our memories and act as our guide, motivating us. They bring us to certain crossroads in life where we have no option but to make a choice. How we deal with these junctions of life, how we respond to them, what we learn and understand from the journey that has brought us to them, the choices we make at such crossroads, make or break an individual.

To make the right choice in life, I always remember a story I had heard from Bhagwan Rajneesh.

A poor old man lived with his grandson in a village. On his grandson's eighteenth birthday, the old man used his life's savings to buy him a horse. The villagers praised the old man for his generosity. The man did not react to these praises. He simply said, 'Do not judge.'

A few days later, the grandson fell from the horse. He was severely injured. His leg had to be amputated. The villagers criticized the man for his stupidity in buying a horse, wasting his savings. The old man did not react to this criticism. He simply said, 'Do not judge.'

Then a war broke out with a neighbouring province. All young men from the village were drafted. The grandson could not go to war as he had only one leg. Again, the villagers scolded the old man for his stupidity. He simply said, 'Do not judge.'

The war was lost and many young men were killed, while a few returned badly injured. The villagers wept for the lives lost. Then they praised the old man for his generous birthday present to his grandson. It had saved his life. He simply said, 'Do not judge.'

This story has helped me cope with every difficult and unpleasant moment of my life. It is my daily energy drink! In moments of despair, I just remember the moral of the story and repeat to myself, 'Do not judge.' It is what helped me deal with the darkness of the thirty-nine months in prison that I served under a plea agreement with the US government.

Most people have a limited understanding of my legal situation. Preconceived stereotypical notions and scandal-mongering have overshadowed the truth. I have been subjected to constant scrutiny, sensationalism and scandals for over thirty years now. I have been tried all these years by public opinion— the media has over and over again indulged in character assassination.

I have faced my life with dignity and courage, and moved on in a creative way, imbibing the lessons from these trying times. I have not dwelled on self-pity, hurt and pain. I have not blamed anyone for my difficult days. I have taken full responsibility for my life with Bhagwan and thereafter. I have learned to disregard others' opinions, approvals and disapprovals, likes and dislikes. I am immune to it all! I live my life in the paradise that I have created in Switzerland. It faces the formidable mountain Sonnenberg. I am content with my work, my communal life and the ups-and-downs of life in general. Nothing shocks me now.

Life is a vast ocean of events. One can either accept what one experiences and learn from the same or keep complaining. To get back on my feet after the hard time I had gone through since I left Bhagwan, I came up with a simple but effective concept: 'Being There!'

I have been busy with my work of taking care of the old and infirm. I missed my parents then as they were in India and I was in Switzerland. Swiss immigration law did not allow them to migrate to Switzerland though I am a Swiss citizen. The residency laws for non-citizens are dependent on health insurance, which is mandatory. However, foreigners with prior illnesses like diabetes or over a certain age do not get travel insurance that covers health costs in Switzerland. My parents were old and suffered from diabetes. That ruled them out for health insurance. Without that, they would never get residence permits for Switzerland even though I wanted them to be near me where I could take care of them. This misfortune motivated me to care for other old people.

I have been working in the field of healthcare for close to thirty years now. I have served hundreds of persons suffering from Alzheimer's, Parkinson's, dementia, schizophrenia, depression and suicidal tendencies. I have also helped several people with severe alcohol addiction problems. I have observed that most of the patients suffer more from isolation and lack of attention. What's missing in their lives is the love and care of people around them. My simple concept of 'being there' does wonders for them.

The foundation of our care home is mutual trust and respect. We are the last resort for our patients who would otherwise be confined to psychiatric clinics. I live with them in the same house and share my room with my sister Mira just as our patients do. We are all on an equal footing. This encourages self-confidence and self-respect. Differences in languages, colour and beliefs do not matter. We are together and we are there for one another. Of course, there are people who still judge me. They label me a cult leader! Doubts over our operations are highlighted over the care we offer. But now I have a thick skin. I am simply myself and ignore such comments. I do not take it personally.

My father often encouraged me to write and speak about my life and experiences. I have taken his advice and opened my heart out in this book. As I look back, memories come flooding back to me. I feel blessed to have met Bhagwan and for what I learned from him. We shared a special bond, and it shaped me into the person I am today. I am proud that Bhagwan chose me as his personal secretary. He helped me discover my potential and made me aware of the massive ocean of energy that exists in me. This knowledge provides a new dimension to my life and its challenges. It gives me courage. It makes waking up in the morning easier. I have learned to enjoy the small things in life. I have always lived life on my own terms and by my own rules.

Rule 2

Everybody deserves a second chance

My father was way ahead of his time when he told me, in 1995, that I had to share my experiences of life. He was convinced that my life would inspire and give people courage. This is why I allow journalists and film-makers to interview me. And that is how *Wild Wild Country* was born.

Wild Wild Country released on Netflix on 16 March 2018. The film, made by two young brothers who had contacted me over email in 2016, documented my time with Bhagwan Shree Rajneesh. It brought about a change in the way people perceive me. *Wild Wild Country* has proven my father's prediction correct. The series has been a critically acclaimed hit and very popular with people from across the globe. I became an inspiration, a feminist and a fashion icon, overnight! I began to receive hundreds of letters full of compliments and praises. Even as I am approaching seventy, living a harmonious, peaceful and comfortable life in Switzerland, having left my stormy and turbulent past behind, after the film I often feel that the past is catching up with me. This time however in a different way. People are feeling and seeing the courage, determination, loyalty and love in me. I am perceived to be beautiful. Believe me, it is a nice change from being considered the epitome of evil as I have been in popular narrative!

Journalists often approach me for a story on my life. However, I do feel that most of them have already 'written' the story before meeting me or hearing me. Not only that, they have even condemned me to hell! They want certain answers from me. If my answers differ from what they want, they distort what I say and use it out of context. For example, a local journalist came to interview me about *Wild Wild Country*. Even though my schedule was full, I made time for him and offered him an interview. Needless to say, within a few minutes I could make out that he was not prepared for me. He seemed closed and unwilling to consider my version of my life. I could see that he had already written his story about my very eventful life and me. One and a half hours later, as I was about to end the interview, he asked, 'Do you make any mistakes?'

I looked at him and said, 'Everyone makes mistakes!'

He insisted: 'But do you?'

My reply to him was clear. 'Yes, I do, and the moment I realize my mistake I correct it.' I added, 'I have learned from my father and Bhagwan that mistakes are the stepping stones of life.'

At that point, one of my assistants came to refill our water. I asked her how she deals with her mistakes.

She explained to him how everyone at the care home was taught not to shy away from mistakes but to look at them objectively and learn from them. No one at the home was ever criticized for making a mistake. She added, 'Sheela is most generous and understanding about mistakes. But she is very hard on herself with her own mistakes! She never hides those.'

When the article came out, it said, 'Sheela makes no mistake. She can never say she made a mistake . . .' I was not wrong. He had written his story before meeting me.

It is rare for people to keep an open mind, be ready to listen, to feel, to understand. Most come with preconceived notions. My sister Mira, who has lived with me for the past twenty years, and has known me from childhood, gets very upset about such prejudiced mindsets. She cannot reconcile the difference between what she sees and feels on a daily basis with what the press reports. She is often annoyed with me for speaking with journalists and film-makers.

One of my team members once asked me, 'Why do you speak with journalists knowing that they are interested only in sensation, scandal and a negative story?'

I understand their point of view. They have to sell their story. Sensation and scandal are saleable. However, even if one reader in a thousand goes beyond the sensationalism and is moved by the deeper, hidden reality, my effort in speaking to journalists is well worth it. I know who I am and no one can change that. Opinions or accusations don't affect me. I accept both hate and love, praise and criticism.

I am reminded of a story Bhagwan often told us about the Buddha. Once, the Buddha was travelling from one village to another with his disciples. At one village, he was welcomed with flowers and sweets. He continued with his journey to the next village where people spat on and hurled obscenities at him. The Buddha wiped the spit off his face without comment or annoyance and continued his journey. His disciples were, however, disturbed.

In the evening, when the Buddha was sitting with his disciples, one of them asked, 'The behaviour of the people in the second village did not disturb you, Bhante (brother)? It made me and the others angry!'

The Buddha replied with a smile, 'The villagers offered me what they had and what they could!'

This beautiful story is what I go back to when faced with false accusations and hate.

Wild Wild Country has definitely altered some of these perceptions. It has drawn attention to my fearlessness, courage, hard work and love. I have received thousands of letters and messages after its release from people who have seen the series, opening their hearts out to me. The younger generation is receptive to these qualities and feels inspired by me. They saw in the film my hard work and dedication to Bhagwan, then and now. They are fascinated with the work we had done in a short span of four years. The city of Rajneeshpuram was built for 10,000 people with complete infrastructure from ground up in a desert of central Oregon. This city was fully equipped and self-sufficient.

Today when I think about it, and what we had accomplished, it scares me. I am amazed. It feels like a dream. It is hard for me to believe that I was chosen to carry out this project and that it happened under my management. When one talks about it or writes about it, it does not seem like a big deal but when you see it in a film in colour, one can't help being awed, much like what we feel when we see historical monuments. Rajneeshpuram and the people who created it have become part of the history of Oregon.

In September 2018, someone wrote to me asking how I was able to successfully persuade people to drop everything and come and follow me; convince wealthy people to donate money to the cause and become our patrons. According to him, the two most important skills a person must have if they are to do extraordinary feats are (i) the ability to persuade people and (ii) the ability to create and tell powerful and convincing stories.

He wanted to know how I did that and if I could share my secret with him to help him deal with his team at work.

When I first read the email, I shook my head in disbelief. I did not understand what he was writing. I felt something was not right. So I forwarded it to my brother Rohit. Rohit is a very accomplished individual. Our father had groomed him personally and whenever we need worldly advice, we consult him.

His short answer was, 'What is this about? I will be cautious with this guy.'

My brother had the same feeling as I did. Feelings are connected with intuition for me and intuition is a process of the heart. I always listen to my intuition.

Out of regard and so as not to disrespect the person who had taken the trouble to write to me, I responded: 'There are no hard and fast methods or techniques that I can offer you on how to deal with your team. I was and I became a part of the team . . . the team became a part of me. I shared my feelings and being with my team. I always prioritized the team. I was there for them. This is the only method I have and I know.'

Rule 3

Love has no limits

By September 1985, my life had reached a point where I had to make a fundamental change. I had no idea of what the future looked like or what I could expect of it! I knew I had to leave Bhagwan and his commune. It was not the easiest of decisions. It required a lot of courage. There would be no turning back. But I had no choice. At stake was my integrity.

I had been immersed in my love for Bhagwan since 1972. He was my life, my inspiration. I still remember the day I first met him as if it was only yesterday. I was visiting Mumbai with my father. Bhagwan lived opposite where we were staying. My father, who always insisted that we never missed an opportunity to learn, took me to visit him.

As we entered Bhagwan's room, he welcomed us with open arms. I sat on the floor at his feet. Looking into his eyes, I felt like I had ceased to be! It was overwhelming. The moment felt eternal. I felt complete. If I had died at the time, I would have not missed life. An empowering love had taken hold of me. From that moment, Bhagwan was the axis around which my life revolved.

Bhagwan invited us to join his evening discourse. It was a special evening for me. We arrived half an hour before the discourse. We sat at the end of the room, leaning against the wall. I waited eagerly to see the man who had created a storm of emotions in my heart earlier that day. All of us stood up to greet his arrival. He passed us, paused and with a sweet, special smile said, 'Come, sit in the front, Seela.' I looked at my father. He nodded and I followed Bhagwan. I sat where Bhagwan had indicated, at his feet.

It was as if there was no one else in the room. Just Bhagwan and me. I saw only his eyes and heard only his voice. I felt he was speaking only to me and resolving all my thoughts and doubts. I melted. When the discourse ended, I simply fell at his feet. He invited us to see him again in the morning.

Soon, I became part of Bhagwan and his ashram in Pune. I started working for him, listening to his discourses every day. The ashram became my new home. As more people came to live around Bhagwan, there was a massive accommodation problem in Pune. We looked for a bigger property in India but we were unsuccessful as India was under Emergency (people could not buy or sell land). Bhagwan decided to move to the US.

Bhagwan's thoughts and the way of life he propagated had a big impact on me. I realized he had a vision. He wanted to unite people irrespective of culture, race and religion. He envisioned a community that would make reflection and self-awareness its goals; that would, through meditation, create a free world, a world that brimmed with positivity. Thousands of people from all over the world participated in this experiment.

This is what Rajneeshpuram was all about. A wonderful experiment for harmonious living based on love and togetherness that attracted people from different countries. No one knew where it would lead us. I supported him unconditionally in the realization of his vision.

Bhagwan had once said: 'Seela came to me like a blank sheet of paper. Nothing was written on her. She was open and empty, and without any prejudices. Immediately she understood me. She completely opened up for me. Seela was perfect. She could repeat what I said to her.' (*The Last Testament*, Vol.1, 30.07.1985).

I had never before experienced the depth of love I felt being with him. It was beyond my imagination. Even after all these years, I have no words to describe how it changed me as a person. It made me realize my potential. It gave me the confidence that I could deal with all emergencies and situations. It made me fearless. I was ready to live life on its terms.

I had only one desire: I wanted to be close to Bhagwan. I visited him as often as I could without being a nuisance. Just to look into his eyes or put my head at his feet or to be near him was heaven for me.

Fourteen years flew by. It was like being on an island; realities outside were completely alien to us. I performed every task Bhagwan gave me. His trust made me grow beyond my limits. I thought, 'If this wonderful man gives me a task, it's because he knows my potential.'

The last few months with him, however, I was at the mercy of a great inner struggle. There were certain activities in Bhagwan's house I was uncomfortable with. Going against his own teachings, Bhagwan consumed drugs. Even though he always said, 'I am against drugs because if they become addictive they will be the most destructive for your journey towards the self. Then you become enchanted into hallucinations.' (*The Last Testament*, Vol. 4, Discourse #6).

There was also his immense craving for luxury goods, which I could no longer reconcile with my values. I was not just his 'beloved Seela' and his secretary. I was also responsible for the community. I was torn within. I loved him so much that I was ready to forget everything—my values, the responsibility and the people in the community. It would have been easy to shut my eyes and continue as before.

Faced with this distress, I remembered the advice of my parents. 'Every person must follow the inner truth. No one needs to be afraid of their feelings.' Their teaching became my guiding light. I knew that I could not compromise with the values they had ingrained in me. I did not want to sell my soul in the name of love. I could not be with my beloved Bhagwan any more. I could not breathe near him any more. It was time for me to leave Bhagwan. I trusted my instincts and followed my heart. I believed that everything would turn out to be fine. I returned all his expensive gifts, which had been an expression of his love, with a goodbye letter.

My parting caused a wave of disappointment and shock. Something no one expected had happened: Bhagwan and Sheela, who had been one heart and one soul, who had stuck together like the sun and the moon, had finally separated. Bhagwan was deeply disappointed in me. My leaving the commune hit him at the core. At the same time, he had to fortify his position in order to retain the trust of his people as many others were contemplating leaving too. Negative stories were spread about me and I was vilified. I had always been aware that many people were jealous of me and wished to be in my place, trusted and loved by Bhagwan. They had the opportunity now.

With my decision to leave the commune, crazy accusations began doing the rounds. Friends and followers of Bhagwan gave vent to their pent-up emotions over me. Bhagwan had always been a master storyteller. The crazy accusations against me were like fire in dry straw and I was ablaze. This fire became the touchstone of my life as well as of his teachings. I was accused of various crimes. I eventually ended up in prison. In my first book *Don't Kill Him!*, I have described this part of my life in detail.

After thirty-nine months in prison in the United States, I understood the essence of Bhagwan's teachings. Bhagwan used every opportunity to train the consciousness and repeatedly created situations in which he tested the limits of our trust and love. He talked about meditation, of love, life, laughing and acceptance, all his life. These are beautiful words and very easy to live by once we are integrated in a harmonious community. Every person can meditate and be satisfied when life is going well. However, alone in a cell, in prison, isolated and rejected by the rest of the world, the true strengths of a human being become apparent. Only negative things were written about me. Hatred and contempt reflected in the faces of the people I met. I did not know whether I would survive the next day or ever see the sun again. These were the darkest days of my life. The only thing that I could do was to find trust and clarity in myself and to accept life as it was.

Despite all the hurtful accusations, my love for him proved indestructible. His teaching was like a precious diamond to me that reflected the beauty of life, without which everything would be empty and dry. Today I am aware that I went through fire out of my love for him.

Rule 4

Build your life on love, patience and acceptance

The time I spent with my parents, the time with Bhagwan and the time in prison have shaped my life. They have made me the person I am today. I was born in 1949 in Baroda, Gujarat, the youngest of six siblings. My parents, Ambalal and Maniben Patel, imparted to me the core beliefs that have stood me in good stead all my life. I grew up in a full house with my brothers and sisters, surrounded by my parents' warmth and laughter. Regardless of the difficulties they faced, my parents always stood firm and never shirked their responsibilities. It has remained an invaluable lesson for me, for which I am infinitely grateful.

Most people perceive their mother and father as separate individuals. For me, however, they are one. They had a special bond with each other. It was almost tangible. Their friends called my mother the engine and my father the carriage. My mother was a bundle of joy and warmth. When she entered a room, her smile filled the space. People ask me where I get my smile from. It is from my mother. From my father I inherited courage and fearlessness. They complemented each other. The sense of oneness that I perceived in my parents' relationship had a profound influence on me; it has kept me grounded and self-assured all through my life.

I saw the strength of their bond and the beauty of their relationship at the time of my mother's death. It was 1997; my parents were living with me in Switzerland. My mother had a medical emergency and I had to rush her to the hospital. My father ran after the car to be with her. He was eighty-six years old. I could see him in the rear-view mirror, running behind the car till we were out of sight, his lungi falling off.

My mother was fully conscious and aware of her situation. She wanted no further medical help. 'I have lived a good, full life. Now you are there to take care of Bapuji . . .' She was ready for death. What was important to her was that Bapuji be taken care of. Her commitment to Bapuji, her love for him was absolute. She wanted to know if my father was around. I sent my secretary to fetch him from home.

My mother said to me, 'Do you have a comb?' She tried to arrange her hair with her fingers and said, 'Is this how Bapuji will see me?' She closed her eyes. She stopped breathing and entered into eternal sleep!

At the age of eighty-three, even with her dying breath, my mother wanted to be beautiful for my father. This sense of love and respect amazed me. They were still deeply in love after sixty years together. I am sure, like other couples, they must have gone through ups and downs in life. But this last moment was filled with the pure love they felt for each other. From that moment on, I could not separate them. They were simply one for me.

My love for Bhagwan was so profound that I do not feel separate from him even though I left him. My departure from his life created a big storm but it did not affect my love for Bhagwan. Through Bhagwan, I learned to perceive life consciously. I blossomed with his love and guidance, and found my true potential.

Prison taught me to be patient. I became aware of how infinitely precious life is. I realized how important love is in the life of every human being. I also developed a heightened awareness of danger. And a sense of my intuition without which I could not have survived. Prison also taught me an important lesson: that everything in life passes, no matter how bad it is. I learned to set priorities on a daily basis. What is important now will not be so the next moment. When one lives in the moment, one can live free of stress. I learned to observe and be present in the moment. I learned to accept the options I had, and there weren't many! I had to become my best friend.

'Matrusaden' and 'Bapusaden', the institutions I have built in Switzerland, lean on three pillars: love, patience and acceptance. When you love, you understand people. When you are patient, you give people the time they need to open up and trust. With acceptance, you can perceive reality and acknowledge it as it is.

Nowadays we are often too busy with ourselves. We have lost interest in loving and caring for others. We are all so stressed that we rarely find the time to smile at someone, listen to them, go for a walk or even dance with them for a few seconds and make them feel, 'I am there for you.' All disease has its roots in isolation and loneliness, in a lack of love. Where there is love, which fosters patience and acceptance, there is bliss.

Rule 5

Follow your dream, and make it come true

I would like to share with you certain aspects of my journey with Bhagwan.

Bhagwan was like a magnet, attracting millions from all across the world. People from all walks of life came to him in pursuit of truth, knowledge and enlightenment. Fed up of their mundane existence blighted by competition and expectations, all of them were looking for something that was missing in their life. Mind you, these were all socially and professionally successful people who nevertheless felt empty, bereft of joy despite their many achievements. They were not in touch with their true feelings.

We arrived at his doorstep looking for answers to the mystery of life and knowledge. Bhagwan offered an alternative to all of us, something we did not have in our life or our environment, something we could not find on our own. With him, we felt we were near the source of knowledge and understanding. He gave us the confidence that we could fill the dark void in ourselves and move forward.

He inspired and motivated us to go beyond the surface and experience our innermost core. Even a menial job became interesting when you were near him. The quality of work changed automatically. New dimensions opened up and you felt pride in what you were doing. One experienced the joy of work, developing a new relationship towards work. Work became sacred.

Bhagwan was in pursuit of his own dream. His vision was bigger than what we could imagine. It would have scared us off had we known about it. We would have laughed at it. It simply would not have fit the limitations of our thoughts. We would have doubted him and everything he stood for it. We were only capable of digesting a drop. His dream was as big as an ocean. Bhagwan had been working on his dream long before I met him. He had seen and studied human nature and psychology. He was well read and an intelligent student. He had a photographic mind and an unmatched ability to analyse any situation. For me he was a genius.

What he envisioned was creating a community of 10,000 self-sufficient and economically independent people without political or economic aspirations who could live together in harmony despite their race, creed, tradition, religion, colour or nationality. He dreamt of bridging all differences by elevating man to a higher consciousness generated through meditation. He wanted us to follow our intuition and inner awareness.

When I met him, I had no such ideas. I did not go to him to learn meditation or spirituality. I was only twenty-one years old, starting out on my life, and had no reason to be fed up of or tired of professional competition. Meeting Bhagwan was a pure gift that the universe conspired to give me, through the agency of my father who always emphasized the importance of learning. I got even luckier; I fell in love with him. This feeling of love overpowered me. I felt surrounded by it. It had no shape, no description. It was simply there—beautiful, real and constant. It filled me with positivity and hope.

He encouraged me to be present at his daily discourses. Of course, I did not require encouragement. Listening to him would transport me to another world. I had never heard anyone speak like him. The sound of his voice was the most wonderful music for my ears. When I was near him, everything made sense to me. I did not have to look for a meaning. It made me feel awake and alert. Watching the expressive movements of his hand and eyes soothed me. His words provided nourishment for the heart. His humour, his logic and intelligence stoked the fire in my mind. It was like homecoming for the soul.

In this state of mind, I was oblivious of his dream. I never wondered what Bhagwan had in mind for me. I was so selfishly in love with him that it never occurred to me that Bhagwan had a dream. He had for years been gathering people around him to carry out his work, his idea. He was not a man of means. He was not from a wealthy family. He hailed from a middle-class family from central India that followed Jainism. He spent his school and university years reading, analysing and discussing with others about his way of thinking.

After finishing his university education, he worked in the same institution as a professor of philosophy. Bhagwan was a popular professor among students. They liked his style of teaching. They were impressed by his logic and knowledge. He offered something out of the ordinary. But it annoyed other professors. They were jealous of his popularity among students. His open, provocative, unconventional and modern approach disturbed them.

Bhagwan's classrooms used to be packed with non-registered students who had heard about him and were curious to hear him. Often, there would be no space left for registered students. Other professors' students were attending Bhagwan's classes and their classrooms were empty. This made them feel inferior. Bhagwan was becoming a nuisance for them. Their constant complaints to the head of the university resulted in the termination of Bhagwan. He lost his job at the university and decided to move forward without a job and the platform it gave him.

Soon he started travelling from one city to another, giving public discourses and conducting meditation camps. Word about him spread and he became known in intellectual circles. His discourses were published as books and audiotapes. Eventually, he moved to Mumbai, where he was received well with his non-conventional approach to the issues of life. Big cities are more tolerant of new ideas. Bhagwan's followers in Mumbai organized an apartment for him in a high-rise building on Pedder Road. His teachings began to gather momentum. In a month, he spoke for ten days during the evenings for one and a half hours from his residence, and ten days at a meditation camp in Mount Abu. One of his disciples in Mumbai offered him land for his headquarters. His first meditation camp was held on this land, and was named 'Anand Sheela'.

Bhagwan had invited Marc, my first husband, and me, to this meditation camp. During the camp, Marc and I were initiated into *sannyas*. Bhagwan named me Ma Anand Sheela— the same name he had for the meditation camp—and Marc Swami Prem Chinmaya. I do not know how he chose names for us. Sannyasins spent much time romancing and creating mysteries with the names. Maybe it was easy for him to choose this name for me as my original birth name was Sheela?

It is difficult to express the enormity of Bhagwan's dream; the vision he had of the task ahead, and the self-confidence and trust he had in himself. There were no blueprints on paper.

He was simply chipping away at the mountain every day. People near Bhagwan were oblivious to it even though he was dependent on his followers for financial and practical support.

Some people ask me about how I was able to persuade the followers at Rajneeshpuram to do almost anything I wanted; how was I able to get them to work tirelessly to build an entire compound, to donate money and time. The only thing I can say is that it was no gold rush. I did not have to sell, persuade or convince anyone to do anything, nor did I ask anyone to donate money. If people gave money or service, they did so of their own volition. Because they believed in Bhagwan's vision. He had been working on it for years before my arrival. He had been answering their questions for years relentlessly, without tiring. He encouraged his listeners to move away from the boundaries of religion, race, etc., and become individuals. Bhagwan's movement was no commercial venture. It was a gathering of people with similar ideas. No one was forced or manipulated to be part of it. All of us wanted to be near Bhagwan and we felt lucky to be there. We considered it our good fortune. We felt like the chosen ones!

I never felt that he and his people were doing all this for money or power. Whatever we did was only out of our conviction and love for him. I felt a sense of commitment and responsibility towards him and the work he had assigned me. I did not want to fail him, ever. We participated in his work because it was fun. It was nice to be around young travellers from all over the world. We felt like we were in the centre of the universe, near the source of something that quenched our thirst, though we seldom understood what it was. We felt free from within.

We did not measure work in terms of time and gain. Work was a form of expression of our love for Bhagwan and an opportunity to be near him. We were never paid for the work we did. We were motivated to do any or all work. There was no work that was big or small. We needed no techniques for motivating us to work. We were proud to be accepted as workers. If you hoped to enjoy the community around Bhagwan, you needed to be a worker.

If his project was only about money and power, it would have been a failure from the start. It would not have been an experiment of collective creativity. Bhagwan had created around him and in us one purpose, the purpose of being together. Creating an energy field through meditation, our conviction and trust in Bhagwan motivated us to carry out our project. Philosophies and knowledge were only reference points from the past. Personal conflicts dissolved on their own and work became the focus of our life. It became our pride and priority.

Let me give you a sense of the daily routine we had at the Mumbai and Pune ashrams, which were the crucibles in which Bhagwan's dream was forged.

A small group of people lived in his apartment at Pedder Road. These included Bhagwan, Vivek, Yoga Chinmaya, Narendra, Kranti and Rupsingh.

Laxmi, Bhagwan's secretary at the time, lived nearby in her family home. She handled all administrative matters for Bhagwan. He carried out his projects through Laxmi. She managed all printing and publication endeavours too. She received guests and visitors, and made appointments for Bhagwan. She entertained Bhagwan's donors.

Vivek took care of Bhagwan's personal needs. Yoga Chinmaya and Narendra transcribed his Hindi discourses and edited his books. Yoga Chinmaya also conducted meditation camps on Chowpatty Beach for Bhagwan's followers in Mumbai. Kranti cooked and did the household chores. Rupsingh was his bodyguard.

Laxmi would arrive early in the morning. Visitors would come between 9 and 11 a.m. Lunch was served between 11 a.m. and 2 p.m., followed by siesta. Bhagwan met visitors again between 2 and 6 p.m. This was followed by public discourse at 7 p.m. either at Bhagwan's apartment or in Azad Maidan. I have attended discourses in both these places. They were unbelievable experiences. When he was in Mount Abu for the meditation camp, the schedule was different. He conducted meditations himself. It was a very enjoyable retreat in his presence.

At the Pune Ashram, Bhagwan lived in Lao Tzu House. He had two rooms, one for his personal use and one for Vivek. Next to these rooms was Laxmi's room, which I shared with her for several years. The room upstairs was given to Greek Mukta. She was an important financial donor of Bhagwan's and had bought the property at 33 Koregaon Park in Pune. The rooms located in the garden were occupied by Mukti and Divya, who cooked for Bhagwan. Kirti, Chaitanya Bharti and Narendra, the Hindi transcribers and editors, also lived there. Kirti was Laxmi's Hindi secretary who answered all the Hindi letters. After the discourse at 8 a.m., Bhagwan worked with Laxmi. Then he spent some time reading every day.

Many people accused Laxmi of being on a power trip as she was the one Bhagwan had made responsible for everything. She approved or disapproved an idea or a project depending on Bhagwan's wishes. People thought that her ideas were impractical at times. Little did anyone know that these were Bhagwan's ideas. Having been a secretary of Bhagwan for several years, and meeting Bhagwan with Laxmi many times when she was his secretary, I can say without hesitation that Bhagwan was the boss. He chose and gave direction to our projects and ideas. Laxmi or I were only executors of his will. The execution had to be done exactly as Bhagwan wished. If we had a conflict with what Bhagwan desired, we presented our thoughts with great respect but the final word was Bhagwan's.

Even when he was in public silence for around 5 years, all decisions that I took were according to him. He saw a number of people during his silence regularly every day. His silence did not mean he was isolated. There is a big misunderstanding in the public mind about Bhagwan's silence. His silence only meant he was not giving public discourses.

Bhagwan never took 'no' for an answer. And in that he found in Laxmi and me willing followers who would go the distance to actualize his vision. Both of us were exposed to constant criticism from his people, his community, mostly from men. Some male followers of Bhagwan felt that if men would be in charge of decision-making, things would be better. Bhagwan, however, felt that women were more intuitive; in his opinion, they were rooted in their heart and therefore more capable and committed to their feelings and work. As women's minds are not invested in ego, and they possess the caring nature of a mother, the energy levels of women are definitely better. Their 'yes' has more readiness. This positive 'yes' changes the quality of any work. It makes work more fun.

When I think of Bhagwan's journey, I feel I benefited from his hard work and abilities. He had already prepared the ground for us. He imbued us with an intuitive practical understanding of our situation. This was my biggest source of strength. I felt equipped to deal with any situation or emergency. It gave me confidence and my confidence was contagious. Being there for him was my biggest secret. It built trust in others and trust opened communication, helping me understand others better. All I can say is: be true to yourselves and to what you wish. Be motivated and remain positive and open. Hold your inner values intact.

As things panned out, my integrity, my inner value would not allow me to compromise Bhagwan's drug use. My departure from Bhagwan landed me in a cesspool of legal trouble. I was arrested in Germany in 1985, and a new chapter opened in my life. However, though I had left Bhagwan's commune, his teachings enabled me to cope with the darkest days of my life.

Rule 6

Always remember, 'This too shall pass'

After my release from prison in 1988, I went to Germany. I had no desire to prove my innocence or take revenge. My family was far away from me and I stood there, all by myself. The only thing that mattered to me was getting out of the crisis. I wanted desperately to move on.

My lawyer, the man I had learned to love so much over the last few years, lived in Germany. I was in love and we had shared many beautiful moments together after my release from prison. I moved near his home and his office so we could be close by. He already had a girlfriend and was finding it difficult to move away from her. He felt guilty about spending time with me, and this caused much emotional strain for both of us. He could neither explain his feelings for me to his girlfriend, nor could he confront me with his emotional conflict nor deal with his guilt.

Once, we planned a trip to Malaysia. When his girlfriend found out, she hid his passport. He could not meet me at the airport as planned. Meanwhile, I had checked in. I ended up travelling alone. I should have understood what direction our relationship was taking. But I was not ready for yet another failure in love. I was yet to overcome the trauma of prison and now I was spending my days waiting for a telephone call from my lover. The waiting almost killed my spirit. It was a disaster.

Trying to cope with the situation, I decided to cross the border of Germany to Switzerland. I thought it would be a good distraction to engage in some shopping. On my way back, I was stopped at a German border checkpost. I was not allowed to enter Germany and was given no reason why. My heart sank. Since my imprisonment, I had often experienced such feelings. It was unsettling.

I wanted to look into the future to see what lay ahead for me. I wished I had a crystal ball; but life does not offer such comforts. I did not have a crystal ball but I had a golden key: Buddha's wise words that I had learned from Bhagwan. 'This too shall pass!'

Today I can say that I am thankful things like a crystal ball do not exist. If they did, I would never have known the resources I had at my disposal. My willpower, my instinct for survival. I would have taken the easy path to deal with my legally complicated and messy life.

It was time for me to move on. In 1989, I made my way to Portugal, via France as I was very close to the French border. There was no border control between Switzerland and France. I found myself a small pension, spent a couple of nights there, then headed to Portugal. I rented a little, half-constructed house in a eucalyptus forest. I lived simply and economically. My cost of living in Portugal was about 50 German marks per month.

I lived the life of a hermit till I left Portugal for Switzerland. A message arrived from a journalist through my lawyer to go underground as I was in danger.

In spite of being emotionally crushed, I tried to keep myself occupied. Being alone was a gift. I was not responsible for anyone else. I only had to take care of myself. It was a relief. I lived in the village of Paderneira, two kilometres from Nazare on the Atlantic coast. I did not speak Portuguese but I managed to survive. Unfortunately, no one in the village spoke English. I had bought an English–Portuguese dictionary to take care of the basic communication involved in buying eggs and bread at the local shop.

The owner of my hut rented rooms for tourists. When he had English-speaking guests, he would call upon me to translate. Not that I spoke good Portuguese. It was only with the help of my dictionary that I was able to communicate. I was known as Senora Englesa in the village. One morning, the owner called me to translate from English to Portuguese. To my surprise, the two men I was to translate for turned out to be two police officers from Oregon. I was surprised that they did not recognize me.

What luck! This gave me hope; perhaps Existence did have a plan for me. It gave me courage that my legal situation would not cripple me. I badly needed something positive to survive. A few days later, I met a young Japanese girl, Mayumi. She was twenty-five and a writer. She had taken a year off from her life in Japan to write her novel. She was having a difficult time in a place that she had rented. I asked her to move in with me. She was happy to do so right away. It helped us both. We developed a close friendship. Even today, I am in touch with her; our friendship has survived the test of time. It was encouraging then and heartwarming today.

After three quarters of a year, I again received a warning from my friend that I was in danger. There had been further accusations against me in Oregon. This news got me worried, and I decided to go to Switzerland for my safety. I did not know what lay ahead of me. It was like walking in the dark but I did not wish to give up. I was desperate and hoped to finally find peace and protection.

On my way to the US to study at the age of seventeen, I once flew over Switzerland and had been fascinated by the beautiful Alps; I had, in my heart, decided to live there one day. This wish came true now. I packed my things and took a bus to Switzerland. I arrived in Basel in the middle of the night, expecting to meet my boyfriend. I did not know that I was in for another shock. After hours of waiting, I realized that he would not come.

I arrived in Switzerland to a new crisis, though Switzerland was a safe place for me. My second husband, Dipo, was Swiss. Through him, I had obtained Swiss citizenship. Switzerland does not extradite its citizens. My reality was grim. I had only 100 Swiss francs in my pocket, no friends, no relatives, no place to stay. But I know that even if I had friends or relatives, my pride would not allow me to bother them with my difficulties. I was emotionally and physically exhausted.

Deep within I knew that everything in my life was happening at the right time in the right place. First, I had to find work and a room. At the age of thirty-eight, I started from scratch. Gradually I let my inner feeling guide me. What work could I do without understanding a word of German? My heart was heavy. Out on a walk in Basel, I sat on a bench under a tree. I noticed a signboard for an employment agency. I went over.

A young woman at the agency understood me and was helpful; she asked me to come back in the afternoon because she had to get some clarifications. On the other side of the building there was another employment agency, which arranged an accommodation for me in a women's shelter. When I went back to the young woman in the afternoon, she offered me a job to work with her grandparents. They were looking for someone to take their dog out. I would be paid 10 francs a day.

I was relieved. I could survive for the next few days. The young woman helped me fill all the forms which were important to be able to live in Switzerland. I liked her from the start. I could pay the costs for the overnight stay in the women's shelter with my first salary in Switzerland. I had a roof over my head, a clean bed and a shower. I shared the room with another woman. This was far more than what I had in prison.

My first walk with the dog was a real adventure. I did not know anything about animals. The dog plonked itself in the middle of the street and refused to move. Cars came from all sides and sounded their horns. I did not know what to do. I begged the dog and said, 'Please come, Barry, please come to the other side with me.' People looked at me and pointed their fingers at their foreheads. They surely thought to themselves, 'This woman is crazy, doesn't she know that she can just pull it over on the leash?'

The dog was my guardian angel. It helped me to survive. Barry and I became friends. He let my heart blossom after all the hard times I had been through. Meanwhile, I kept looking for work because I could not survive on this salary. I had always enjoyed caring for others, so I thought I could work as a housekeeper. As soon as I made the wish, it came true. The old couple whose dog I took out was looking for a housekeeper to live with them, because their present housekeeper was pregnant. The couple spoke English, which made it easier for me to interact with them.

Finally, after a long time, a semblance of normality returned to my life. I was paid 16 francs an hour. I slept well and had enough to eat. I felt safe with the old couple. The man was a lawyer and was always ready to help me. It was time for me to leave behind the hardships of the last few years and recover. I enjoyed the work I was doing. After paying for the health insurance, telephone costs and some cosmetics, I was able to save quite a bit. I was a frugal person and very careful with money. During our evening conversations, the couple often talked about the fears of getting old. I began to understand the problems of old people.

After eight months, it was time for a change. We parted as friends. While I was eagerly looking for work again, I could tell by the reactions of the people that they knew my face from the media. None of them had ever known me personally or spoken to me, but nobody was willing to give me a chance.

Meanwhile, I was longing for my parents and my daughter; I had not seen them in more than three years now. I wanted to bring my parents to Switzerland as soon as possible. When I was in prison, I saw my daughter regularly. She visited me often. She lived with my brother Rohit and my sister Maya and went to school and to university in the US. Now she is forty-six years old and is a mother of a daughter. We are in regular contact. We have an understanding that when she is not doing well or is hurting, she must connect with me.

Rule 7

Accept life as it comes

In 1990, I came across some information that would help kick-start my new life and career in Switzerland. Apparently, a law allowed one to take in up to five people in one's house and care for them. I did not know whom to contact to verify its accuracy. I asked an acquaintance of mine for more information. He called a state official and confirmed that what I had heard was indeed correct.

I rented a house and set it up for three elderly persons to live with me. I had no training or much technical understanding of nursing care at that time; I did not think I needed that either. I had seen my mother look after our father and us. I had also seen my mother take care of poor people near our farm in India. Moreover, for fourteen years, I had looked after Bhagwan and his community, without any training, education or special expertise. The one ingredient one needs when it comes to caring is to understand the needs of others. I was sure of two things. First, I knew that you care for others in the same way as you would like yourself to be cared for. Second, being there for others is the key in caregiving.

While setting up Bhagwan's community in Pune and later in Rajneeshpuram, I had come up with the idea of providing services like restaurant, spa, medical centre, garments shop, gift shop, hotel, school, airport, bank, and so on. I had then gone ahead and implemented the same. Through these services, we provided comfort and security for our commune members and visitors. It was a clean, quality service at a fixed, reasonable price.

I had enough ability and experience to assess the needs of my elderly residents. I set up my house without any frills in a very short time, first for three people, which expanded to three more after three months. I had structured myself to function alone as I did not have the luxury of hiring people to help me. There was no capital to start a big project. I started the commune with a small sum of money saved up from working as a housekeeper for an old couple in Basel. Emotionally too I was not ready to deal with others.

I paid the deposit for a month and a month's rent in advance on the lease for the five-bedroom house. After this, I was left with 1,500 Swiss francs for furniture and basic food to begin with. I was proud of setting up the house within my meagre resources.

Someone's misfortune often becomes another's fortune. That is exactly what happened with me and my first resident. An eighty-year-old woman, Mrs R, had been asked to vacate her apartment—three villages further up in the valley from where I was starting a commune for seniors—where she had lived for twenty-six years. Her daughter lived 200 metres from my house. That is how she came to know about my project. She was looking for a place for her mother urgently. The old-age homes available were costly. The woman's son could not keep her, and she did not want to go to the daughter, who was happy to take care of her, as she was in the process of divorcing her husband. She did not approve of her daughter's divorce. The day she had to relinquish her old apartment coincided with the opening day of my commune. Mrs R moved in with me. She was my first resident.

This enabled me to pay the rent for the next few months, which had been a big worry for me. As I started out rebuilding my life, I wanted to take baby steps. I had no fancy budget projections or great ambitions. Just a steely determination. I had informed the neighbourhood doctors and hospitals about my home. They welcomed the idea. They thought it would be good for the neighbouring communities. I had finally found something worthwhile and something I enjoyed doing. I hoped it would fill the emotional void in my heart in the absence of love and my parents. This was an opportunity to get back on my feet. I wanted to relieve my parents of worries over the hard and difficult days I had experienced since leaving Bhagwan.

A few days later, a man in his mid-sixties brought his eighty-eight-year-old mother to me. Mrs L had just had a tumour the size of a melon removed from her stomach. The doctors had given her a few months to live. Her son had already planned the funeral arrangement. As it turned out, she lived under my care till she was ninety-six years old. Mrs L had swollen, blue feet because of poor blood circulation. Between my daily foot massage, and a natural medicine for the stomach, I managed to remove the excess water, and the swelling reduced. In a short time, the circulation in her feet improved.

After three days in my care, she asked her son to move her into my home permanently. At that time, she was already living in a catholic old-age home in a nearby city. She had another disabled son who had been mentally impaired since birth. He had lived in an institution in Basel for twenty-five years. Once

Mrs L moved in, he became a regular visitor to our commune, visiting her every weekend and enjoying lunch with us.

The local hospital sent me my third resident, an eighty-six-year-old woman paralysed from a brain stroke.

Gradually, I started picking up information about the illnesses that I was dealing with. If I did not understand something, I would ask local doctors to help me. I consulted books and dictionaries. Thirty years ago, I did not know Mr Google! I was a quick learner. My mother would say, 'Use your common sense and that will take care of many problems.' How true! Common sense is the most reliable support during emergencies.

Slowly but surely my own little commune was beginning to take shape far away from Rajneeshpuram. I was busy with it from morning till evening. I would come down to the kitchen at seven to pick up my watered-down black coffee, and Mrs L's breakfast tray. I would help her get out of bed, walk her to the bathroom, prepare her toothbrush, wash her face and eyes, and then help her with her bathrobe. Bring her to the desk in her room and help her sit comfortably to eat her breakfast.

Next, I went to wake up and shower Mrs G. She was paralysed on one side and could not stand or walk by herself. She needed help with each step. I taught her how to hold the banisters with both her hands and move. I would be with her and help her through this. I then took her back to her room, walking behind her and helping her by gently pushing her from the back. I would bring her to the kitchen, where she would sip her coffee and wait till I showered. Then, Mrs R and I would both come down. The three of us would then have breakfast together listening to music at the kitchen table.

After breakfast, I would take care of Mrs L, help her shower and bring her down. I would then go up to clean the bathrooms, make the beds and finish the daily chores. By 10.00 a.m., I would start preparing food. Mrs R was very happy to help me with the salad or in cutting some vegetables.

After lunch together, I would help the ladies to their beds for the afternoon rest. After that, I would clean up the kitchen and take care of pending things. At 3 p.m. I helped them out of bed and brought them downstairs for coffee and snacks. After that, we went for a short walk for fresh air, some simple, good exercise for old people.

I made sure that they had a minimum of two litres of water to drink in a day. Normally, old people do not like to drink much. They avoid using the toilet as they are not stable on their feet. Another reason they do not feel thirsty is that they eat bland food. With my cooking, they did not have that problem.

The ladies also became my German-language teachers. When I started the commune, I neither spoke German nor did I understand a word of it. I felt their needs and wishes intuitively. They appreciated my help and I was grateful that they offered me an opportunity to get back on my feet. It was important for me to speak German; I had to grow my roots in Switzerland.

I was feeling better about my situation but new worries started eating away at me. Would this work hold me financially stable? I would spend hours worried about the cash flow. I did not need much for myself, but would my new venture survive? I would again and again remind myself to remain positive and continue with my work.

It was time for me to know myself, cope with my situation, and understand my new life. Having led a hectic life so far, I started feeling that I did not have enough to do! The afternoons when my residents took their siestas made me feel restless. I had the energy and time to take on a bit more to do. Just then, I read an advertisement in a magazine about how to start a small business from home. The only thing I needed to set up this business was a fax machine. I was able to manage a fax machine within my budget. It cost 900 francs, which was a worthwhile investment even if the business did not work out. Meanwhile, two more people joined my home and the cash flow improved. By the end of the year, the number went up to six.

I successfully launched a company and named it Anuja Impex. I ran it from my house in the afternoon. The risk I took in purchasing the fax machine paid off many times over. Now I was fully occupied with my work. I was clear that I did not want to be a victim of my circumstances nor make excuses for the rest of my life. I had learned from my father to face difficult situations in life with grace and dignity without blaming or pointing fingers at others. 'Learn from all situations,' he would say. No one forced me to be with Bhagwan; no one forced me to leave Bhagwan. It was my choice. Now I had to face the consequence without complaining.

During those days, my daughter Anuja was visiting me on vacation. She was around fifteen or sixteen at the time. She felt that I was not the same 'Sheeli' she remembered from Rajneeshpuram. For a young girl to notice this difference affected me too; she interpreted this change in me to mean that I did not love her. I had to explain to her that I had a very tough life since I left Bhagwan. It was still hard for me to understand and accept all that had happened. It could perhaps take my whole life to make sense of it. My daughter was right. I was not the same Sheeli. I had grown from within . . .

When I thought about it later, I was proud of her observation. Anuja's insight was the result of her deep love for me.

Rule 8

If you believe in it, your wish will come true

India had become independent a couple of years before I was born. My father was deeply involved in the struggle for independence with Mahatma Gandhi. He had spent four years in prison, fighting for India's independence. Bapuji's prison time was a badge of honour for him and all of us.

In our home freedom was worshipped; it was synonymous with responsibility. Bapuji had encouraged us children to think independently and respectfully from an early age. He paid a lot of attention to our education. He gave us the courage to remain true to our thoughts and feelings. He emphasized the use of intellect and logic. There was this song that he would sing to us every day. It exemplified the virtues of being alert, aware and conscious.

Of course, these words did not mean as much when I was young as they do now. His words started resonating with me after I met Bhagwan. They began to influence my behaviour. What had been mere words earlier were now imbued with deeper meanings. I understood them intuitively in proximity to Bhagwan.

My parents never asked me anything about my situation, about prison or the charges I had faced. Yet I could feel their deep pain within. They had accepted my fate with such grace and dignity that it made me even more aware of my responsibility towards them. I had to get back on my feet and remain healthy, physically and psychologically.

At this juncture, I was not interested in fighting the world or in responding to the media. I had to free myself of others' opinions of me. I had no time, resources or energy to waste on such futile fights. I had to focus on my freedom, away from any further entanglement with the law. I was alone. I was my best friend. I could not afford to be distracted from my goal of rendering Ba-Bapuji free of their deep pain due to my situation. My priority was clear to me.

Ba-Bapuji supported my hard work with pride and joy. They eagerly waited to visit me for three months every year. Three months were too short a time but we made the most of it. We spent quality time together. I was grateful to see that Ba-Bapuji were feeling relaxed. They believed that my life was coming together again.

In a short time, the commune was full. I cooked and cleaned, washed and ironed, and nursed my people. It was a 24/7 job. I did all the work myself. I had to be aware of my time and my priorities. I had to optimize my energy. I could not afford to fall sick. Hiring others was not financially viable. I made it a point to learn from and use the experiences I had had to deal with whatever unpleasantness I encountered in the present. It became a game for me. I was getting better at dealing with my complex past and its crises.

No one bothered me about my past; I did not hide it either. I was proud of it. I thought that the public would have finally lost their interest in my sensational, scandalous story, now that it was old. Little did I know. One morning I got a call from a prominent newspaper. They wanted to interview me for a story on communes for senior citizens. I agreed. I thought it would be good publicity for my venture. I recalled Bhagwan's advice. When people criticized us for bad press, he would say to me, 'Seela, remember there is no good or bad press. All press is good. It draws the reader's attention. It is a free advertisement. Advertising is expensive . . .'

The journalist was about my age. I gave him a tour of my house. He interviewed me for two hours during which I spoke about my work at the commune. I gave him my card and told him that he could call me if he had any more questions. He left looking happy. He had not recognized me. He had not asked me about Bhagwan or my life with him. I wondered whether at last my past had ceased to matter.

Soon, I forgot about the interview and got busy with my work. One evening, I was getting ready to fall asleep when the phone rang. It was not normal for someone to call at 9 p.m. The Swiss are very particular about not disturbing someone at this hour. I wondered who it could be.

It was the journalist who had interviewed me.

He said, 'As I was writing about your home and looking at your visiting card, I felt I knew the name from somewhere. I am not sure . . . Are you the same Sheela . . . Bhagwan's secretary . . .?'

I cut him short. 'Yes, I am the same Sheela . . .'

He was polite. He apologized for disturbing me so late in the evening and added, 'I have to tell you this; now that I know who you are, I cannot do the story I wanted to do originally about your commune for the elderly. I will do a Saturday feature about Sheela and Bhagwan; this will be the main feature for two consecutive Saturdays . . .'

I protested. It was unfair. Old people and their communities needed more attention. It was an important story to talk about and draw reader's attention to. But clearly, for the media, the story about old people was not as sensational as a story about Bhagwan and Sheela!

I wondered what the fallout of the feature would be, how it would impact the peace and quiet I had nurtured over the last few years. I decided to face it head-on, and for a change I did not have the sinking feeling I used to. I took it as a gift from Existence.

Two full-page feature stories came out on two consecutive Saturdays, with a big spread of photos. The cat was out of the bag. Not that I was hiding anything, but I wasn't trying to draw attention to myself either. A number of other stories followed in different local newspapers and magazines. I continued my work without letting all this affect me. If someone in the neighbourhood was curious, I responded as best as I could without complicating my story. The Swiss are very accommodating. If they do not like something, they ignore it. Confrontation is not their style! My neighbours left me alone.

Existence, however, in all its munificence, seemed to have a plan for me through this journalistic episode. One rich Swiss from our province, Canton, saw an opportunity to profit through me. He had a big villa two villages from where I lived and worked. He wanted to enter into a partnership with me. My instinct told me, 'No partnership!' Bapuji had once said to me, 'Sheeli, never get involved in any sort of partnership; you will be always misunderstood and taken advantage of.'

Though I did not get into a partnership, I took the opportunity that came my way. I rented the villa. Over the next one and a half years, the number of residents went up to sixteen. The local doctors were happy with my work. They saw a real need for my home and appreciated the quality of care I offered. The local hospitals and psychiatric clinics were happy to refer patients to me. Most of my patients came through them and through word-of-mouth publicity about my work. To see a smile on my residents' faces made all the hard work worthwhile.

There had been a substantial rise in the number of elderly people in Switzerland and the rest of Europe. Old-age homes did not have enough beds to accommodate this increase. I did not know much of what was going on in the world around me as I was too busy trying to keep my feet on the ground. Language was a barrier and I had no time to read or catch up with the news. I was unaware of new laws being created to address such issues. I lived a fairly isolated life with my residents. This isolation had been good for me. It helped me cope with the emotional upheavals and turbulence I had been through. It was my refuge, and I felt safe and secure in it.

I had no contact with any government body related to social institutes. I had a permission to do business as an individual. I had taken care of all tax, insurance and other regulations necessary. One evening, I got a call from a person who was the head of a small home in our province. I did not know him or his institute. He told me about a meeting and a press conference with a head doctor from the government in charge of all old-age homes. An announcement was made regarding approved homes and institutes in Canton, which would be eligible for financial support from the state and the federal government.

He told me, 'You were not there. It was an important meeting. Your home is not on the Canton list . . .'

Local journalists confronted the head doctor about it. My home was full and always remained full. Why was I not on the list?

The doctor had apparently given a bureaucratic answer, which typically meant nothing. 'There is no need for those beds in projections of required beds . . .'

The journalists persevered. 'All her beds are full and there is no need for them?'

Soon after, another homeowner visited me. I got calls from local journalists. They wanted my reaction about the head doctor's comments. I did not have much to say about it, as I had not fully understood the issue. Nor did I know what the head doctor had said, as I was not there. I was not depending on any government money either. As long as my beds were full, I did not require the government's financial support. Of course, I needed to pay bills and survive but I had not started the commune to earn money and become rich. I was doing this only for the love of my parents.

Even with my limited understanding of German, I realized that the journalists were pointing at the discrimination against me. I attributed this to my past with Bhagwan and my prison term. However, I did not take it personally. I was not ready for a conflict. I was content that they did not disturb my work. In fact, I was grateful to them for ignoring me for their own reasons. Later, I found out that they had the home listed under my first name 'Sheela' instead of the official name. Perhaps I was on their mind more than my institute.

The government left me alone; they never informed me about new laws or information related to the field till 2001. Looking back, I can say that I am grateful. By 2001, I had founded another house, 'Bapusaden'. Between the two homes, I now had about thirty-six residents.

During this time one important immigration law was passed. According to it, all residents of Switzerland would get health insurance in spite of their existing illnesses and age. I was thrilled. I felt that the law had been enacted only for me, to unite me with my parents permanently. As I was a Swiss citizen, under this law my parents could migrate to Switzerland immediately.

I filed the documents with the department of immigration without wasting time. Within six weeks, my parents were with me. My isolated, cold life was filled with sunshine. Existence had made my wish of caring for my parents in their old age come true.

Over the years, all my wishes and desires have been fulfilled directly or indirectly. As such, I am very careful in making a wish. I try to be vigilant that no negative wish comes to my mind, lest that too comes true.

Rule 9

Face challenges with all you have

I lived like a hermit with my residents. I continue to live in the same way. I keep myself active and busy. I do not have much time or desire to be social. Yet I live a full social life with my residents. I plan activities and events with them but I do not have much to do with my neighbours.

I was happy to have my parents with me. It was blissful, sipping morning tea together, joking or playing cards with one another in the afternoon. To be able to roll a few chapattis for them and serve that to them hot as they ate was pure joy.

I was however being tested on all fronts. I had sixteen residents at the time, my parents and two Labradors, Lalla and Rajab. We called them Lalli and Raji lovingly. The majority of the residents suffered from Alzheimer's and dementia. My work was demanding and the hours long.

When I rented the big villa, I had a verbal agreement that the owner would secure the premises with a fence around the garden to protect our residents. He had also agreed to build proper banisters for the staircases, besides carrying out a few small repairs. Despite repeated verbal and written requests, the owner failed to fulfil the agreement for over a year; he simply ignored it. It was becoming dangerous for my residents without the fence. As they were patients of dementia, if any of them strayed out, they would not know how to cross the street or in fact find their way back home.

I had no choice but to go to court. The court gave me the right to cancel my contract but I would be required to vacate the house in three months. My lawyer was not sure. He wondered if I could find another place in such a short time. I gave it a thought and replied, 'For Bhagwan and his people I could find a land for a new commune in seven days . . . this is for my people and me . . . why not? If Existence desires for me to move forward, I will find the new house and the strength to manage it.'

I had no idea what I was getting myself into. To find a big house that could accommodate sixteen residents was a mammoth task. I had no financial backing. Given my public image, it was unlikely that any bank would give me a mortgage.

However, if Existence tests you with trying circumstances, it also sends you its angels to hold your hand. Susanna was one such special person who supported and helped me. I met her first in the summer of 1996 through my publisher for *Tötet Ihn Nicht*, the German translation of my book *Don't Kill Him!*. Susanna was the translator.

Before we started working on the book, I had requested the publisher to arrange for the translator to come and stay with me so that she could get to know me, how I use language, what different words mean to me, how I think, how I feel and how I deal with my daily situation. I wanted her to know me for who I was. Only then could she interpret my writing and translate it into another language.

Susanna accepted my invitation. We finished the work in two months. We became friends during this time. She was very good with language and writing. She had a knack for technology and computers, something I had no affinity for. She was also good at bookkeeping and office work.

After the book was published, she continued to live with me for five years. She was aware of my legal and professional situations. She got to know my residents well too. She took on a number of responsibilities on her own. She seemed to be having fun and I could see that she was enjoying her time at the commune. She dealt with a number of crises on my behalf. Her help and support came at a vital time in my life. I trusted her fully. I had no doubts that she had come as a divine intervention in my life.

Susanna was with me when I went to court against my house owner. At that time, I wasn't well-versed in German. She helped me prepare all the necessary documents for court. Thereafter, she played a key role in helping me find a new house, dealing with problems arising from the purchase of the house and preparing for the move; she was my backbone. There was never a shortage of crises in my life and Susanna was right beside me during those five years.

Finding a big enough house was not easy. Having wasted the first four weeks in looking for a house in the wrong areas, I was desperate to find a house soon. I was getting nervous, as I had no plan B. If I could not find a place in three months, what would I do? Where would I go with all my residents? I soldiered on, firm in the belief that Existence had something good in store for me. I told myself, 'Sheela, if you have not found what you hoped for, it's only because you are not clear about what you want, and you are not looking in the right direction . . .'

This helped me to relax. It gave me my confidence back. The next morning we renewed our search. The house was waiting for us. It was in a village bordering Canton Baselland and Canton Aargau, on an isolated street up a small hill on the outskirts off Maisprach. We found out that it was a restaurant-guest house. Not only that, it used to be a Michelin restaurant owned by the famous chef, Chez Armin! It was rumoured that Armin had lost this property and the bank had taken possession of it.

I was delighted. After a few telephone calls, we found out which bank was dealing with the property. It was the same one with which I banked. There was, however, more struggle ahead. My first challenge was the price. I knew that nothing came cheap in Switzerland, especially property. Rental was not possible as the bank wanted to sell and recover its investment. As it was a big property, the bank wanted 40 per cent of the value in down payment. I had nowhere close to that kind of money. I also had to be mindful of my working capital requirements.

It was time to give myself another pep talk. 'You bought a property for Bhagwan for US$ 5.9 million without having more than US$ 50,000. Now you have to do it for yourself; you are in a much better position now.'

I arranged a meeting with my banker to explain my situation and to convince him that I was a serious buyer. I would try to raise the needed capital for the mortgage. But first I needed the key for the house. I had very little time left, and I needed to start preparing the house for us to move in. I knew that no one would give a key to their property to a stranger on a word of honour. And with my scandalous past I was surprised they would even talk to me. I convinced the banker to accept 50,000 Swiss francs, all that I had, and allow me to work. If I did not raise the money needed for the mortgage, the bank could keep the money!

This was a gamble but I took the risk. I started work with Susanna to renovate the bedrooms. We started ripping out old dirty carpets glued with silicon to the floor. Our hands hurt but we continued to get the house ready before the deadline. I was no longer young but I was determined. I was tired to my bones physically and emotionally fraught as my mother had passed away just three months ago. My father was sad as his life partner and soulmate was not around him. Seeing him suffer made me sad but also gave me the strength to go on. I knew that if I achieved my goal, he would feel better. His pride in me was my capital.

After fifteen days, I was able to raise only 20 per cent from my brothers and sisters. Susanna wrote a thank-you letter to the banker from me. I took the letter and the key to the house to the banker. I told him, 'I am sorry, I have managed to raise only 20 per cent of the money which is already waiting in my bank account as you know. Here is the key and an explanation of my failure to raise more money.'

The banker discerned my honesty and sincerity. Existence came to my rescue again. The banker asked me to wait. He went to his boss and came back with a new condition. He made me a new offer. He would accept 20 per cent but I would have to bring two co-signers from our region for 100,000 Swiss francs each. They had to be citizens of Switzerland. This was even more difficult for me. But it was understandable for the banker.

I did not want to say no right away without trying. I did tell him that I had no contacts other than my doctors and the families of my residents. I could not ask them; it would be unprofessional. But I would try my best. I did not know who to ask and who to contact. I was not social. I had no friends. The only people outside the house I knew were my optician and a politician.

I thought about it over two days. Then I made up my mind to act on it. I asked the optician first; I felt he trusted me. Then

I asked the politician. To my surprise, both said yes. They were both moved by my struggles. The trust they both offered changed our relationship into friendship. I was grateful to them both, then and now too. In my heart, I thanked Existence for the miracle. I put into action what I had learned from my parents about responsibility and priority; before the year was out, I repaid the bank to free my two co-signers.

During the purchase of the house, Susanna helped me with all necessary documents, reading them, explaining them to me. Without any help, the two of us renovated the house. This involved deep cleaning, laying 348 sq. m. of floor tiles, and painting the whole house. We had no money to hire expert constructors who could do the job. We didn't have time to engage a construction-renovation company who would take six to eight months, even a year, to complete the renovation. It was good that we did not have the luxury of excess money.

We were happy with what we had accomplished. We managed to meet our deadline with the court by handing over our rented house to the owner. During the last week of November 1997, we moved out of the rented villa into our own house, overlooking the famous Sonnenberg.

It was Existence's gift to me, enabled by Ba-Bapuji's blessings and Bhagwan's training. My father named this house 'Matrusaden' in honour of my mother. In 1998, I named my new old-age home 'Bapusaden' in honour of my father. It has been over twenty years since 'Bapusaden' came into being. It is our little palace.

Rule 10

A daily routine provides discipline and structure

There's nothing scientific in the way I deal with residents at Matrusaden and Bapusaden. I approach it intuitively, letting my heart lead the way. I have tried to recreate the same environment and conditions for my residents that my parents did for us, provide them with the same love and care, the joy and spirit that I felt at my childhood home. Unrest or worry had no place at my parent's home; it was like living in a paradise of peace and security.

Some people ask me why I have so many photographs of my parents around my home. My parents are my inspiration; they guide me, provide me with strength. It is like having a statue of the Buddha in a room, transmitting peace and tranquility. The same way my parents bring universal joy and fearlessness.

My methods are non-conventional and practical. My systems are proofed by the government. We have created an approach that goes beyond a quality management handbook. I have a team of caregivers who look after the residents with love and a sense of purpose. The daily routines and structures are designed to suit my residents. I reach out to them. They do not have to comply with my needs and bend to my structure.

This simple understanding takes the stress out of the initial period of adjustment for a new resident. The flexibility of our approach works well with patients suffering from dementia and schizophrenia.

There are certain simple daily routines the residents are expected to adhere to. They are assigned small tasks to learn the importance of living in a household. These give them a sense of fulfilment and joy. They learn to be there for others in a small way. Mornings are occupied with breakfast and showers. This is followed by a mid-morning one-hour walk. After lunch and siesta, residents engage in therapeutic activities like painting, music, dancing, social and mind-training games, etc. In the evenings, they go for a walk or spend time on the fitness machine. Dinner is followed by some time with the TV or music. Then it's bedtime. Over weekends, we have spontaneous short day trips. We go out shopping, or venture out for coffee and cake. We do make changes in the activities as per the wishes of the residents. The basic structure however remains the same.

It does not always work smoothly, of course. There are severely depressive, difficult, aggressive residents with borderline personality disorders. They have problems with any sort of structure or authority. They want to provoke you. They watch how you react. Are you afraid? Judging them does not help. Here, they must perceive the strength of your character, your self-confidence. If they feel you are afraid, angry, or disgusted, you have lost the battle of the ego. No cold professional words help in these extreme cases.

Recently, we had a resident with complex behavioural issues. She was aggressive, foul-mouthed; she would hit, spit on others. She had been through several homes and came to us under a court order. We were the last refuge for her. I took it up as a challenge. I thought to myself, if Existence has sent her to me, I had to accept it as a gift. Through her, I was reminded of my strengths; she was a test of my love, trust, dedication and commitment towards my team and residents. One day, she threw something at Mirjam, my secretary. If Mirjam had not ducked, it would have hit her in the face. I intervened. She continued her verbal attack on me. She spat on my face. I did not budge. Neither did I lose my cool. As her spit dried up in her mouth, she stopped and went into her room. My non-reaction became the best response to her aggression.

During and after this event I thought many times about the story of the Buddha being spat at. I understood the meaning of the Buddha's story through this episode. I discussed this event in detail with my team. It was a profound learning experience for all of us. It taught us how to deal with such charged situations without taking things personally. My residents are my teachers. They have made me the person I am today.

One needs self-confidence, deep understanding and the patience of an elephant to care for the residents. It requires the utmost respect for their individual rights. In the beginning, just to motivate them to walk is like trying to move mountains. It is important to move them into activities naturally. If it looks or feels too structured, you are likely to fail. For instance, they help unload the car when I return from shopping for provisions, set or clean the dinner table, peel vegetables, prepare coffee for in-between mealtimes, or help with the drying up of the dishes. We try to draw their attention to each small task as an important one. These keep them occupied. However, these activities must be integrated organically into their daily lives. They must look and feel like fun than rather chores. Humour and playfulness help.

I lead by example. They see me work long hours every day. My office desk is right in the middle of their sitting area.

They see me enjoy what I do. They have fun being with me and the team. Any activity that is forced could have disastrous results, particularly given the psychological states of many of my residents. If they work for hours in a noisy, unfriendly atmosphere, it will cause them immense stress.

It is important to understand their needs. Not just their basic ones like food and shelter but also psychological ones. They need to be encouraged to engage in activities that bring joy and enhance their inherent talents. This will provide them with self-respect and enable them to look at life beyond their disabilities. It is important to treat them not as disabled, but as individuals with their own abilities. The group dynamic during joint activities gives them new confidence, a new energy. It infuses them with courage to try things they were shy about before. It gives them a feeling of belonging, of being there for each other. They feel safe and secure in a group.

There is no reason for us to label them or make them feel inferior. We try to integrate them into the day-to-day rhythms of life. We eat the same food as the residents. We dress ourselves in comfortable and informal clothing. Our visitors cannot differentiate between the team and the residents. The residents intuitively feel this. When they see us exercise, they are also motivated to do so. They realize that rules and discipline are not just for them. Everyone around is subject to the same.

It reminds me of a story about a Zen master that Bhagwan once told me.

A mother went to a Zen master to ask guidance for her young son. She sought help from the master saying her son ate too much sugar, to the point of ruining his health. She had tried many remedies without any success.

The master heard her problem. He asked her to visit him again after five weeks, with her son. She could not understand

During summer vacations in Baroda
with my sister Maya in 1961

Twelve-year-old me participating in
an interstate Garba competition in
Ahmedabad

(Left to right): Satish Kalelker, my mother, sister Maya, Kakasahib Kalelker,
fifteen-year-old me, my father

My older brother, Rohit, and I skating in Verona, New Jersey, in 1969

On a date with Chinmaya
(Marc) in New Jersey in 1969

With Rene, a neighbour's child, in
New Jersey in 1969

With Chinmaya in New York
State in 1970

At the Newark Airport with Ba and
Bapuji in 1972

With Ba and Bapuji
at Tandalja Farm,
Baroda, in 1973

With my nephew
at Tandalja Farm,
Baroda, in 1973

With Chinmaya in Baroda,
in 1973

My sister Mira shaving my head in 1973 at the
Tandalja Farm, Baroda

At the airport in
Belgium in 1974

In a discourse, waiting
for Bhagwan, in Poona
(now Pune), Maharashtra,
in 1974

At the evening darshan with
Bhagwan in Poona in 1974

At the morning discourse
in Poona in 1974

At the evening darshan with
Bhagwan in Poona in 1975

Relaxing at the
Poona ashram in
our room in 1976

In a discourse and waiting for Bhagwan with Chinmaya at the Buddha Hall, Poona, 1978

Poona, 1976

With Anuja (daughter) after I left Bhagwan, in Sonnenhalde, Blackforest, Germany, in 1985

With brother Bipin in 1986 during my time in prison

In a bus from prison to the Los Angeles airport after my release in December 1988

In the airplane after my
release from prison in 1988

With Ba in Baden-Baden,
Germany, after prison, in 1988

With Bapuji after
prison in 1988

January 1989 in
Zurich, Switzerland

With Ba at the new old-age home in
Hölstein, Switzerland in 1991

With my rabbit in Maisprach,
Switzerland, in June 1998

With my two dogs, Lalla and Rajab, in
Maisprach, Switzerland, in 1998

At Anuja's wedding in Maisprach,
Switzerland, in 2005

At Anuja's wedding in Switzerland with
Rekha, Maya and Mira

why the master asked her to come again. He could well have told her son to stop eating sugar. She was confused. However, she accepted the Zen master's request to come after five weeks. She visited the Zen master again. After some small talk, the Zen master told the son, 'It is not healthy to eat sugar. I too do not eat sugar for my good health.'

The boy understood. The miracle happened! The son stopped eating sugar. The mother could not believe her eyes. A few days later, the woman came to thank the master. She wanted to know the secret of his miraculous words to her son. 'Kindly explain to me your secret. I have been to so many doctors for help. No one could stop my son from eating sugar. You asked me to return after five weeks. You could have told him to stop that very day, when I visited you the first time.'

The Zen master laughed and said: 'There is no big secret. How can I stop your son from eating sugar, when I eat it myself? After you came to me, I stopped having sugar for five weeks. Now I could tell him to stop. He followed my suggestion because I do not have two standards, one for him and one for me.'

If I like good coffee for breakfast, maybe my people would like the same too? The day must begin well for me, my team and my residents. A cup of good, strong coffee with friendly small talk helps pull residents out of their morning slumber and puts them in a positive frame of mind. As soon as I come to my workplace, I put on some music that everyone enjoys. Music is important as a mood enhancer for people who suffer from depression. Visitors to our commune often comment about our happy, joyous atmosphere: 'It is different! Even from the parking lot you feel a special vibration . . . and then you come out, with your big welcoming smile . . . it is special.'

We work with many different illnesses. It is rare for us to refuse someone. We do that only when we do not have the proper facilities to address the illness. We love to work with elderly people. We have residents suffering from suicidal tendencies, aggression, borderline personality disorder, alcohol addiction, anorexia and trauma. The one area I prefer not to work in is drug addiction as I personally don't consider it an illness. I regard it as an illness of choice. Addiction alters the character of an individual. Addicts become self-centred and manipulative. They have no respect or regard for others. They do not care for their environment and the space of others.

Sometimes we get drug addicts as residents without our knowledge. At times we are not given complete information and history for fear that we might refuse admission. It happened recently when a home brought us one of their residents. They were not able to deal with him. We were told that he was quiet and polite. I should have wondered why he needed to be in a home if he was so good. Or why the other home needed a new place for him.

After he came to us, I noticed that he kept visiting the nearby city of Basel. On his return, I found him behaving strangely. His eyes were not normal. He made different excuses for his outings. One day it was a visit to his psychiatrist, another day his mother, his grandmother, etc. Upon his return, he would not have his dinner. When I questioned him, he showed me a bag of sugar jellybeans. It was almost empty. Something was not right. The first morning in the shower, my nurse had noticed that his back was full of pimples, big and small, with white pus in them. We started to notice every little detail about him. Asking him was a waste of time, as he never said anything that was coherent.

It didn't take us long to realize he had a drug problem. He would drink cleaning liquids, aftershave and perfume, if he could get his hands on them in the house or elsewhere. When confronted he would deny it. He found newer ways to deal with his addiction. He would take magazine covers that were heavily embossed with silver and gold or other metals. He would burn them with CDs, and sniff the smoke and ashes for a high! We tried our best but it was impossible to handle him or get him to mend his ways. Eventually, he moved to another institute. We were complimented for engaging with him for over four years.

I owe the success I have with my residents to the fact that I enjoy what I do. I am inspired by the love I feel for what I am doing. For example, as I write this now, I am not concerned whether it will be successful or not. I want to write what I have learned and share my experiences with my readers. This is what inspires me. Just letting myself run with the words makes me feel lighter in my heart. It is a beautiful feeling. This moment is my success, it is all that matters.

Rule 11

Sex and sexuality are natural

It was my intuition that told me to leave Bhagwan in 1985. Today, thirty-six years later, I must say my intuition, this gut feeling, has served me well. Leaving Bhagwan was the right choice for my being and my work. With logic and reason, one uses intuition less and less. We tend to become calculative and feelings become secondary. One thinks instead of feeling. As a result, intuition is disappearing from our lives and the understanding of the heart is diminished. Life is then filled with doubts and scepticism. Intuition is based on love and trust. Today love is polluted with doubts and scepticism. How much do we value love in our lives? Here I remember an incident that took place in my life decades ago. Chinmaya, my first love, had complained to Bhagwan about me.

Chinmaya said, 'Bhagwan, it is so strange that whenever I am with someone other than Sheela, Sheela shows up on the scene! She has no way of knowing that I am with someone else; yet somehow she does. I do not understand how . . .'

Bhagwan laughed and replied, 'It is intuition. Seela loves you. Her love is so deep that she will appear from nowhere . . .'

Chinmaya and I understood each other. Our deep love and respect for each other bound and liberated us.

*

When your partner seems disinterested in you, you take it personally. You feel ignored. You feel rejected. You feel alone, isolated. You feel something is missing in your life. This deficit, this feeling of isolation, this lack of interest is what I call the 'black hole of love'.

In love as in life it is important to be honest with ourselves about our relationships. It does not matter in what relationship you are. Clarity is needed to avoid confusion of feelings. Such confusion will only lead to false expectations, disappointments and depression.

For me 'love' is another name for 'being there'. You are there because you care for your partner and others. You are there because the other means something to you. You feel connected, liked and welcomed. The feeling of care and connection is what carries the soothing feeling of 'love'. By 'being there' I try to reduce lack of love in others' lives. It is a long and constant process. But it is my experience that it does start filling the black hole. It happens because I take my people for what they are at face value. I do not judge them. I walk up to them instead of waiting for them to come to me. I show them how important they are for me. I let them know how they have enriched my life. I give them respect. I treat them no less than I treat myself. I am their mirror and they are the same for me.

The word 'love' and its feelings are often confused and misunderstood in the world. Most of us try to classify 'love' by declaring it as motherly, sisterly, brotherly, for a lover, etc.

Why this classification? I assume the classifications are there to avoid the misuse of this divine, sacred, vital feeling of the heart.

Love is often associated with 'sex and security'. In love, relationships and marriage one often comes across the confusion of love. Sexuality and security play a major role. We choose to remain in broken relationships or unbearable conflicts only so that we have emotional and financial security. We put up with all kinds of treatment and compromise what we believe in; to hold on to the other we are ready to sell our souls and betray ourselves, put up with injustice and bad behaviour. We choose comfort over love. No wonder then relationships become a burden and bring depression. The 'black hole' becomes part of our core.

Love has become synonymous with sex. It is important to understand this very sensitive and misunderstood subject of sex and sexuality. It disturbs everyone in society. Everyone has an opinion on sex. But most are afraid to talk about it openly. Religions around the world have restricted and at times viewed sex as taboo. Different social norms have placed restrictions on sex or created rules and regulations around it for reasons of their own.

I want to talk about this theme with gratitude to my father, mother and Bhagwan. They gave me a healthy and humane understanding on this subject.

When I left home for the first time, away from my parents, to the US for higher studies, my father talked to my sisters and me for days and weeks on different subjects. He prepared us for our upcoming adventures in a foreign land, inculcating in our minds strength and clarity of thought.

One of the important subjects he spoke about was sex and sexuality. At first, it felt strange to hear him hold forth with such frankness. Until this point in life, this was an aspect no one had discussed with us. Father and Mother had taken care of us with love and care. Father explained to my sister Maya and me, 'Ba (mother) and I will not be there to look after and guide you now. It is important that you understand a few basic things. You are of an age where young men will be attracted to you or you might get attracted to them. It is normal and natural. Do not think that you have to get married to the first man you meet. You don't have to think that Ba and I will look for a husband for you.'

He continued, 'Meet young men of your age freely. Make friends with them. Be open to your feelings. Do not hide them. Express them. Maybe you would wish to express those feelings and engage yourselves in physical contact. These are natural and normal feelings. Do not be afraid of such feelings. Do not be shy about them. Do not think that you are bad because of such feelings. Try to understand them and be very careful in expressing them.'

He asked us, 'Do you understand?'

We answered shyly, 'Yes.'

He continued, 'Don't settle down and marry the first person you meet. Before deciding to marry, date, go out with different persons, and then choose your partner. Remember sex is neither bad nor dirty. Just try to understand your feelings of sex and its needs. Your feelings matter just the same as your partners'. Find someone who respects you, and is compatible with you.'

He added in a stern voice, 'Never allow aggression and disrespect in any situation from anyone. Especially in matters of sex . . .'

From that moment, those words of wisdom were carved in my mind and heart. Even today they ring in my ears sometimes. I was in awe of my parents. My father's vision was so clear and the depth of my parents' understanding was unbelievable. No school would provide such training. Only loving parents can do it.

To add to this, my life with Bhagwan and his teachings filled the gaps I had missed in my understanding of sex. Bhagwan taught a whole new dimension of choice in sex without being judgmental. Bhagwan's teachings made sexual freedom devoid of emotional guilt. His teachings took sex out of the moral bonds of marriage and relationships. In his understanding, the pleasure of consensual sexuality is not a sin. In fact, he elevates sex and sexuality to its pure status of tantra and spirituality.

This healthy training from my father and Bhagwan gave me a deep understanding and insight into sex. Bhagwan made no difference between homosexuals and heterosexuals. He believed that both have their own freedom of sexual choice, and both should be respected and accepted equally. Transsexuals also have the same choices and deserve the same respect as any other human being. We are all humans; we all have sexual needs. We have to understand and learn to deal with them.

People are often afraid to show their sexuality directly as they are afraid that they will be judged wrongly. Anyone who shows interest in multiple sexual partners is labelled promiscuous. Aspersions are cast on their character. That's why they don't speak about it or feel ashamed to speak about it. Such people are not accepted by our society. They invite judgement and criticism.

Our sexuality is attached to our ego. Sexuality guided by ego and domination becomes offensive for both parties. One must have the courage to say 'no' in all relationships, in all situations. You must express yourself and say no if you do not wish to participate in sexual activity with your partner. It is your right to deny it. Compromise will only make things worse for you and your partner. Such compromises can bring deep depression, anger and hate because you are going against your instinct and intuition. It is against your heart and soul.

Not just in sex, you should follow the same principles with regard to other feelings too. You should be able to make and express your choice in all relationships. By saying 'no', you are not being disrespectful or negative; in fact, you are being honest with yourself and your partner.

In Bhagwan's community, discrimination and stereotypes had no place. After some time with Bhagwan, we forgot differences of age, colour, nationality and language. We spoke about sex and sexuality openly, without feeling guilty or ashamed about it.

This reminds me of a story about one of my residents, S. She was in her mid-seventies and was disabled from a brain operation. She had lost all awareness of social norms and inhibitions. Her vocabulary was filled with indecent sexual terminology. It did not matter if she was talking with a resident, or the team, or a total stranger. My house is frequently visited by journalists. My residents mill around as I speak with visitors. I introduce my visitors to my residents. During one such occasion, I introduced S to a journalist.

S started talking to the journalist. 'Last night I fucked seventy-seven men,' she said, and started laughing. I could not help laughing with her—no her joy was so infectious. I did not correct her or condemn her. It did not disturb me. I knew that she had been in psychiatric clinics for eleven years. In the world she inhabited, she was a happy soul. She meant no disrespect to anyone. It was the illness that caused such behaviour.

The journalist was shocked. I explained to him about S and her behaviour. I also spoke with him about how Bhagwan and his people have been labelled as sexual degenerates. Bhagwan did not teach us to be promiscuous. He simply explained: be conscious of your feelings and understand them. Have a healthy approach to sex, our basic instinct.

For me S's behavior was not disturbing. What is alarming is the aggression and perversion that exist because of a lack of understanding and education of sexual feelings. Suppression of these feelings is dangerous. Religions suppress sexuality by preaching celibacy. They are the breeding ground for aggression and perversions. A lot of so-called religious and pious people are perpetrators of such crimes as we have seen across the world.

Sexuality in our homes

Looking back, I feel I was well prepared to deal with issues of sexuality among my residents. We have strict rules around sex and sexuality in our homes. Any physical or sexual contact between residents and the working team is forbidden. This is a chargeable offence. No excuses are accepted and no sympathy offered if this rule is broken. This automatically also becomes a police case.

Our open, transparent living and working environment naturally deters unwanted and unlawful situations. My training of openness and trust gives a healthy understanding of one's own sexuality. The team is well trained to be aware of such events and reminded to follow their intuition by being conscious.

In our homes, residents can express their sexual feelings towards one another and can engage in sexual activities with mutual consent. Sexuality is a need of the body. It has to be lived and enjoyed. One should understand it rather than being ashamed or afraid of it. One can speak about it freely in trust. We do not taboo sex or sexuality. Suppression of sex or its feelings causes massive psychological and mental problems.

It can alter your character. It can make a person perverse and violent. One should engage in sex only with the consent and respect of the partner. It should be a positive act where both parties are fulfilled. Sex should not be a burden.

It reminds me of a beautiful story of the Buddha that Bhagwan once shared with us.

Two disciples of Buddha were returning from a journey. They had to cross over a small river. In the evening hours, the currents were strong. A woman was sitting under a tree near the bank of the river. She was troubled. She did not know how to swim and the waters were higher than they had been in the morning when she had crossed this river. She was afraid of wild animals stalking the area at night. She needed to cross the river.

She was happy to see the two disciples of the Buddha. She requested them to carry her over the water to the other side. She explained her worries and told them she did not know how to swim. She needed help.

The older disciple said to her, 'I apologize. My religion forbids me from looking at or talking with a woman as I am an ascetic. I cannot help you.' He went ahead and crossed the river without her. He felt he had exercised his non-sexuality well. He waited on the other side of the river for his companion to cross over.

To his surprise, he saw his younger companion crossing the river with the woman on his shoulders. This made him angry beyond all reason. The young companion dropped the woman on the other side of the river, wishing her a safe journey home. This was too much for the old disciple. This sacrilegious act was unacceptable.

They went to greet the Buddha. The Buddha asked the older disciple the reason for his unhappiness and anger. The old man explained how the young companion had behaved. Not only had he touched the woman but even carried her on his shoulder. He had gone against the religious order. Buddha then heard the young disciple's version of the story. He explained, 'If I would not have helped her, she would have become a victim of wild animals this evening. I had compassion for her helplessness. I put her on my shoulder and helped her cross the river.'

The Buddha declared to his disciples that the younger disciple had understood the meaning of being a true ascetic. He had realized that his sexuality was not a burden for him. He did not have to run away from his sexuality. He had acted and responded correctly. He transcended his sexuality into compassion.

Similarly, our residents don't have to hide or run away from their sexual desires. At the same time, we try to draw their attention to the critical aspects of sexuality. We teach them by not treating the subject as taboo. We create trust and confidence in them so that they can talk about their feelings of sexuality openly with us. We don't make them feel guilty of such emotions. I believe there is no heaven or hell to be condemned to! They are taught to articulate and say 'no' to it, if they do not want it. This open communication builds trust among residents and renders the environment free of ugly, inhuman displays of sexual violation. It is clear to everybody that sexual abuse or misconduct will not be tolerated from anybody.

We encourage residents not to use sex as a currency to obtain material favours outside our homes. We give them an understanding of hygiene and disease-oriented information. We explain to them about the dangers of sexually transmitted diseases.

There are often problems with residents with an addiction. They only understand their addiction. They are oblivious to everything else. So, when we get a resident with an addiction issue, we work very closely with their guardian to tackle the same with the consent of the resident. I have had a number of such cases. Through awareness and observation, and without judgement, we are able to find out such traits and habits of the residents. One simply has to be there with open eyes and ears.

I had one alcoholic woman, fifty-six years old. She was placed in our home as a 'hopeless case'. Within our structure, we deal with difficult and problematic people well. In the first three days, we realized from where she got the extra money to drink herself to death! She used to engage in sex in toilets at the train station. She also confirmed it. Another resident had been involved in sex in protected disabled workshop toilets. They would go anywhere to earn a few extra bucks to fulfil their addiction.

It is sad. It is at times unimaginable. But it is how it is.

We have a resident in his fifties. On his first visit to us, we knew that he was not what he had been presenting to us. He had lived all his life with his father in a house, isolated. He spoke in whispers. It was difficult to understand. I felt he was afraid of talking. The father had died recently. His family was not ready, or was not able to care for him. The social help department asked us if we would offer a place for him.

We had a place free and he needed a place urgently so we took him. We rarely reject someone. The next day he moved in with us.

The first week went well. We felt that he was a bit nervous. We interpreted his nervousness as a result of his new situation and that perhaps he was missing his father. It was important for us to understand him well and quickly, to make him comfortable in our home.

A few days later, he was spotted completely naked in the hall. We ignored it as we thought he was trying to provoke a reaction or was testing our limits. The caregiver went to him and simply told him to put on his clothes as other people live in the house. He followed her instructions without resistance. Next, he was seen masturbating in the garden. Now it was time for us to respond. This response had to be very human and professional. I went personally to explain to him. I explained without judging him, 'It is legally not allowed to masturbate or to expose yourself in public. You can masturbate in the privacy of your room or in the bathroom. You should know that if you continue like this, someone can file a police complaint against you.' He heard me and understood.

We had no history on this resident. There was no information about him. When the resident comes from a psychiatric clinic, we get some information to work with. But this was not the case with him. We informed a psychiatrist about his behaviour. We have a very competent and sympathetic psychiatrist whom I have known for close to a quarter of a century. He was one of the chief doctors of an external psychiatric clinic. He is our in-house psychiatrist as well.

A few days later, the resident became more aggressive and nervous. With the help of the psychiatrist, we succeeded in stabilizing him. He was able to speak more clearly in a very short time. He began opening up and finding his wings. He does not feel oppressed here any longer. His aggression has a lot to do with unfulfilled sexuality. We make sure he does not disturb others with his sexuality.

It is important that the team does not approach issues of sex and sexuality with hesitation, or with stereotypical social attitudes towards the residents. One has to tackle such issues with much sensitivity and understanding. If it disturbs you, the resident will pick up intuitively that you are afraid of talking about it. Then it can go in the wrong direction. The discussion can bring confusion instead of clarity. You have to be very professional and direct about it and avoid beating around the bush. To bring this understanding one must function collectively and this understanding reaches out to all in our commune.

Rule 12

Accept the opportunities that come your way with an open mind

I never had any plans to expand my venture in Switzerland. I was simply accepting life as it came my way and I was content with it. I did not judge nor did I demand that things be a certain way. I had only one focus. I needed to be independent and self-sufficient. I worked hard without expectations and looked forward to the small pleasures in my daily life. Being on my feet became my mantra. This clarity made my life simple.

Every day was a new special day. I accepted the day as it came without judging or interpreting. I took it at face value. These were small tricks to make my life easy. They kept me and my surrounding positive. My worries about my future were lessened. I was so busy from morning till night that I had no time to think and worry about my past.

On most days, I would be physically exhausted by night. It was a good feeling. It gave me a good sleep but also energy for the next day. I was available 24x7 for my residents. I never felt burdened by my residents even if they needed me in the middle of the night. I would thank Existence that I was there to deal with the emergency. It is the same feeling I have today. I always remind my team, 'We have this well-paying work because of our residents; we should always be thankful to them.'

*

In 2009, I started a project in Vietnam. One of my team members in Switzerland, Fu, was Vietnamese. After having worked with us for a few days, he said to me, 'You know, Sheela, we do not have homes like this in Vietnam.'

I laughed and said, 'Then we should start one in Vietnam, Fu.'

Fu was from Hanoi. A Few days later, we went on a trip to Hanoi. I had never been to Hanoi before.

Hanoi did not work for me, as I did not feel comfortable in a big city. The big city is not my choice for a small project. So we returned from Hanoi. A few weeks later, my secretary Heike and I went to Ho Chi Minh City. We looked at a number of properties to rent but I did not find any suitable. About six months before this, I had vacationed with a part of my team in Mui Ne and liked the region. Heike and I decided to visit this area again after looking at Ho Chi Minh City. We both felt at home there. It is strange how one feels at home in certain places and not in others. I have had these kinds of feelings throughout my life. Such feelings are related to intuition which I do not ignore.

We decided to explore opportunities in Mui Ne. Before we began our journey to Mui Ne, I had contacted some real-estate agents to see if they would arrange to show me some properties. It was difficult. Most of them did not speak a word of English. I managed to get across to one person. As I understood, someone would wait for us in Mui Ne at the Hotel Hawaii. I doubted if I had understood, but when you are drowning even a straw comes handy! On the way, Heike and I discussed my understanding of the situation. Heike could not help as even she does not speak English.

I thought to myself, 'We are so spoilt in the Western world. We have become self-centred. We expect the whole world to speak the language we understand. We have no tolerance of others. We complain that they don't speak English or German. But we never ask why we don't speak their language.'

I had to immediately check myself from such one-sided expectations. It helped me handle the irritation I felt about not finding someone to speak English or German to explain my needs. This is something I strive to do whenever I feel there's something unfair. This helps communication with others. It discourages arrogance in me. We arrived in Mui Ne. We looked for Hotel Hawaii. To our surprise there was a young man waiting for us. I was hopeful again. The man however did not speak English. My hope seemed to fade away. However, I was not ready to give up. One can substitute language with expressions of hands, eyes and feet. Just then a beautiful young woman, Hoa, appeared. Hoa means a beautiful flower. She knew a little English and became our translator. It reminded me of my time in Portugal and how I used to translate from Portuguese to English for tourists. With Hoa hope came back!

We saw a property right away and rejected it. The price was over our budget and it did not have enough space. The Next day we saw three old hotels. They ranged from twenty-four rooms to forty-eight rooms. I was looking for a small house for disabled people and here I was being shown large hotels. Out of curiosity, I visited them all with Hoa. I kept my mind open. I thought, why not. One could create a financially viable project. I did not judge. I accepted whatever Existence had in store for me.

Finally, I decided to rent a twenty-four-room hotel for ten years. It was a simple, affordable place frequented by backpackers. Situated right next to the beach, it was an ideal place for my Swiss residents to vacation. Most rooms had an ocean view. My Swiss residents needed a routine and stability, not big hotels, where they feel they would be lost or be afraid. It also would be easier for the team to look after our residents. I weighed the pros and cons in my mind before deciding to rent the hotel. It felt like killing two birds with one stone.

The property had potential for improvement. It was situated in the less developed part of Mui Ne. So the rents were comparatively less. I felt I could manage it even if the whole project did not break even. I had no idea of the laws of the land. Nor did I know the language. Being European, you have to pay surcharges due to local greed. This is something I have dealt with in Vietnam and in Mauritius. In fact, Mauritius has two prices for most things, from taxi to textile and other consumer items—one for local Mauritians and the other for Europeans. These issues however do not deter me. My sister Mira always scolded me, asked me not to be stupid. She always advised me to think hard before taking a decision. You see, I live life by my own rules.

I renovated the hotel in six weeks. I had learned to get projects off the ground quickly. Otherwise, I would lose interest. Life moves at the speed of light and with intensity for me. It was not possible for me, by nature, to be careful and detailed. After living with Bhagwan for fourteen years, I had learned to be spontaneous and live in the moment.

The hotel offered my Vietnamese team a possibility for their future. I am available for guidance to them but now they manage and work the place on their own. We decided to call it 'Matrusaden Residence'.

I feel Existence and my intuition guided me, with a full understanding that it could all fall apart. I have always listened to my inner voice, my feelings. I am certain that as I go forward, the road will open up step by step. But I have to take the first step.

Hoa became my partner in this venture. She was a student and a graduate of economics. I trusted her and she took the risk of partnering with me. For me, trust is not a risk. It is a compliment. With the help of Hoa we set up the hotel. Now, my Swiss residents had a lovely place for vacation; other tourists also had a wonderful, clean, aesthetic place, with a reasonably priced hotel next to the ocean.

Opposite the hotel, about 50 metres away, we rented another house, where we created an eight-bed old-age home for persons in need—old fisherwomen and men from nearby villages who had no one to care for them. Our charitable project was sustained by the hotel. From the profits the hotel generated, we managed to build another place with my guidance. The original core team moved there and continues their life independent of me. Hoa still manages the new project.

The sweet young girls now have families of their own; they have become mothers and independent women in their own right. They now speak some English and feel strong as they stand on their own feet. I am indeed proud of them.

Opportunities come our way every moment. It depends on how we respond to them. I have had much success as I take all that happens in life as an opportunity. This simplifies my life as I do not have to choose. It is there, available for me. Just as being there. A life full of opportunity is eventful. Boredom has no place in such an eventful life. Every moment feels special.

After leaving Bhagwan and the time after prison, I have only known a life of opportunity. With Bhagwan too I had the opportunity to learn and discover my strengths and my qualities. If I had not jumped into it, thinking of my security or education or husband or tradition, religion or any other situation, I would have missed life's jackpot.

I don't say that everyone will have the same success as I have had or that you should be reckless in your choices. In fact you should be aware of the choices and listen to your intuition. Analyse your desires and wishes well. See to it that your motivation is not corrupt or dishonest towards others or your own self.

From the proceeds of this hotel, we built another beautiful small hotel nearby, a little distance away from the mainstream tourist area with views of a coconut forest. This is the bonus for Hoa and the team for working hard and honestly. It offers them a future, a business of their own to move forward in life without depending on anyone. We helped each other and did it together. On their own, they may not have had the possibility to create their own business. I wish them good luck and many more opportunities in their life.

*

My relationship with my oldest sister Rekha had suffered due to the crisis in my life. After I left Bhagwan, my life was not stable. I had to first take care of myself, and then only could I think of the luxuries of maintaining my relationships.

After I left Rajneeshpuram, my whole family was devastated. They all helped me as much as they could and supported me when they could. But I kept my siblings at a distance out of a sense of self-respect. I did not want them to be involved in my mess. They were not a part of my mess. I did not want my family to suffer at the hands of the US government. Firstly, I needed to come out of my shitty situation and then focus my energies into the relationships that were near and dear to my heart.

By 2014, the legal clouds of my past were a distant memory. I had created a home for my residents and for me. I was not on the street any more, worrying where to spend the night. Or how to pay for my next meal. I felt comfortable and relaxed. I had a good team and I could finally take a few days off. Everyone is so used to me that they feel nothing can go wrong with me around. Such is their confidence in me. But now I thought it would be good training for my team to manage the homes without me while I was on vacation.

So I took ten days off in 2014 and I invited Rekha to a vacation with me to Mauritius. She was retired and free of responsibilities. It had been years since we had spent quality time together. I wanted to make up for the lost time. How foolish of me to think that. Who knows what tomorrow brings? But my intentions were in the right place.

As planned, we arrived in beautiful Mauritius. It was truly a paradise around the hotel. We settled in our rooms and then went to the restaurant for coffee and cake. We were enjoying our coffee, looking at the Indian Ocean and its natural beauty.

The waiter who got our coffee asked us, 'Where do you come from?'

When he realized I was from Switzerland, his questioning became more detailed.

I explained that I worked with old and disabled people. I was a founder of a nursing home. While he was digesting my information, I asked him, 'Do you have nursing homes here for your old and disabled?'

'Yes, they are called ashrams here . . .' he replied.

'Ashram?' I repeated. For me 'ashram' has a totally different meaning. An ashram is a place for learning with a spiritual master; it is a community of the master and his students. I did not look for an explanation for it. I asked him, 'Do you know where I could find such an ashram?'

'Just 250 metres outside the hotel on the left,' he replied.

I was interested in knowing how they worked with their old and disabled. I was horrified by the conditions at the first 'ashram'. Our animal stables are much more hygienic. The uncomfortable furniture was old and torn. Only the TV and radio were working. It was a place with eighteen beds. The mattresses had no bed sheets, were overused, unclean and had urine spots. Urine had dried on the floor. I saw a patient walking with urine flowing from him onto the floor. The patients were in a sad and pitiful situation.

I was afraid to touch any of it. But this tragedy touched my heart. I immediately thought of my parents. I asked myself, 'Could I accept this condition of living for Ba-Bapuji?' It made me sad. It was no longer possible for me to enjoy the vacation at my luxury hotel. I thought of my ability to create a new home in a short time, if given the opportunity. I had all the management systems and a lot of experience in this field. I could not sleep that evening. All kind of thoughts went through my mind. My dilemma was that I lived in Switzerland.

One thing was clear to me: if I could not help this situation, I should not complain about it. That is something I have learned in life. If you cannot improve a situation, don't complain. Do something about it. My mind was active.

My sister was eager to help. She was happy to tag along with me and keep herself busy. I spent my vacation going around the island. I found the east coast of Mauritius, where our hotel was located, to be the most beautiful. It was not overcrowded with tourists like the west coast. I was collecting information about Mauritius without knowing the purpose for it. One thing was certain. I was disturbed about what I had experienced in the ashram where people did not even have enough food.

I was sixty-five years old at the time. Whatever I had to do, I had to do quickly. As our trip got over, I bid goodbye to my sister and returned to Switzerland. Convinced about setting up an ashram of good standards for the old and disabled, I headed back to Mauritius as soon as I could. It took me sixteen months to get government permission for a twenty-bed home. Three weeks later 'Matrusaden Residential Care Home' was ready and operational. It has been running at full capacity successfully for five years now.

Before opening the home, I spent three weeks in Mauritius, training my team. I have a team of fifteen persons, including a doctor, an assistant to the doctor and an accountant. I am in daily contact with my team for big and small questions or any other guidance. I visit Matrusaden Residential Care Home every year.

Before I began this project, I visited ten different homes in Mauritius. They were not fit for human inhabitation. The Mauritius government has all the necessary laws and systems in place to avoid these horrible conditions in the disability homes that I had seen and observed. I can only blame the situation on corrupt managers and government officials. The helpless, disabled and old do not have someone to protect them and their rights.

As there was little I could do about ingrained corruption in the system, I tried to establish my own standard. I was just dealing with the problem at hand, the quality and standard of care in a disability home. Our home in Mauritius has the same standard of cleanliness and order as in Switzerland. I put my experience in Switzerland to good use to make the project in Mauritius successful and viable. I am thankful to Existence for offering me this opportunity.

In India, we have a saying that when Goddess Laxmi comes to your home, you do not go to wash your face! Goddess Laxmi represents opportunity and wealth. Prioritize the opportunity that comes your way. Don't waste your time at that moment on other unimportant things. Be open to the opportunity and welcome it. I took the opportunities that came my way and set up two international old-age homes in Vietnam and in Mauritius.

Rule 13

Don't hesitate to speak the truth

For eighteen years from 1990, the homes founded by me were private and independent institutes. As our homes were recognized by the government under a new law, we became part of the Canton's list. It meant that the government now had its say in financial and other matters related to the institutes. It became mandatory for us to participate in and to comply with the new law, or to shut the institutes in our Canton. The government's main intention with this new law was to standardize all homes, exercise financial control, stop corruption and halt ever-increasing healthcare costs. With this new law, the goal was also to prevent misuse of government funds, which had been offered generously to the approved institutes.

All homes have to comply with a tedious bureaucratic system for this approval. This system is organized by highly qualified desk workers, and must be applied, though it is less practical and realistic. We had to go through challenging approval processes and bureaucracy. To fulfil the requirements, as the head of our homes, I have to go to meetings arranged by the local government every quarter.

We had no idea of the new law in 2001. We did not know that it would bring equal benefits to all institutes. The distribution of funds became the responsibility of the Canton, as the federal government stopped the direct allocation of money. To implement these socio-economic polices, it was necessary to apply a new law.

All homes in our Canton are engaged in implementing this new law. In retrospect, I assume that the government did not provide the complete picture of the law change from the beginning so as to avoid panic and confusion among the homes. Instead, they went about it step by step. The new law came into effect in 2008, though there had been indications since 2001. I had thought our existence would not be affected as we were a private home. I was wrong; under the new law all homes had to be approved by the Canton.

Every big and small home required operating permits from the government. To obtain this permit one required extensive documentations. The language for it was very dense and full of legalese. Just this was enough to dry up motivation for the individuals running homes.

The dry, cold, technical language devoid of feelings that is used by the government and bureaucracy is complicated. It is not easy to understand. It requires highly specialized individuals to work it. It excludes many in the work team and is not a language one uses on a daily basis at work. I know none of my residents would understand it. Would it not be easier if we spoke a language that we all understood? Would everyday language make the integration easier? Communication would become simpler and effective. Among our team, we use everyday language to overcome all barriers of communication as we are a multicultural team.

After thirty years in this work, communication with my residents is of utmost priority for me. I speak the language they understand. That is what I recommend to my team. For me the language of the heart is important, meaning we should speak clearly and understandably. That is the respect we show to our residents.

This however does not mean that I am against education. For me, learning is very important. I believe everyone should have basic education with developed thought processes and logic; to be able to analyse is important. Yet, learning from life means much more for me. For me education must improve and enhance life.

I remember my father delaying my trip to the US for a few days, so that I could meet with Bhagwan and J. Krishnamurti, and listen to their wisdom. Some relatives criticized him but my father was not bothered. He knew that what I would learn from a few days of discourses from Bhagwan and J. Krishnamurti would stand me in good stead for several lifetimes. My father was right. The education I received from Bhagwan is evident in every aspect of my life.

The social institute law is a dangerous situation for both the caregiver and the caretaker. It takes the heart out of the institutions. Caregivers will become machines, pressed under time without fulfilment and joy. This will cause many psychological issues for the caregivers and caretakers. No one benefits from it.

The work we do with our residents is successful because they are not just an object of financial calculations or costs. To lower the costs, institutions are forced to be commercial. There is a lot of pressure for the institutions to be cost-effective.

In the beginning it may look like the government has saved millions, but it is only an illusion of numbers. Numbers look real, but the results can be illusory when caregivers start experiencing burnout which can cause actual damages and losses. A single such case affects many. There are hidden costs involved, both emotional and financial. It is an emotional stress for all. It has a ripple effect.

If one wants to avoid corruption in the system, one needs to go to the root of the corruption. One has to educate individuals from their young age with a different set of values in society. Corruption has to be removed from the root. Individuals have to be trained to function with honest dedication. Ethical and cultural values have to change.

Greed has become an intrinsic part of our lives. It is hard to remove greed from an individual. The desire to obtain what others don't have and to be different than others is very prominent in our society, in education, in material and in spiritual terms. One way or the other, one wants to be on top, better, higher than the other. This competitive streak makes it impossible to avoid or reduce corruption.

*

Firstly, we received an official letter that requested a presentation of our concept. We complied with the required process. We waited for a licence. It took three years from the day of submission of our concept. We waited with uncertainty about our existence in this changing environment of social care.

We had our first and formal inspection with Mr Fair, the head of the department in the government. We passed our audit with flying colours. Mr Fair was a serious, no-nonsense man. His approach in improving his department's working ethos did not go down well with everyone. He was not corrupt. His experience had made him tough in his approach to dealing with homes.

I answered all his questions openly. I was transparent. When he asked me about my education, I replied, 'Where do I begin, from the highest or the lowest?'

He replied, 'From the highest.'

Without hesitation, I told him the truth, 'My highest education was in prison. Thirty-nine months in prison taught me patience and the value of time!'

With this, I hit the right note. It was a first step in opening the door for a good start of the audit. Today, we have the reputation in his department of being trustworthy and honest. What we say and agree to, we do. Our concept is unconventional. We were not so happy about this new law, but we had no choice in the matter if we wanted to continue to function in this field. Instead of complaining, we started working towards compliance.

Mirjam took the lead with this work. She has a hidden talent for it. Mirjam is very close to my heart and has worked with me for seventeen years. She is a natural and intuitive student of law. She is not a lawyer but she understands and can interpret the law well. She is a good sounding board for me to test my ideas. She responds as an honest critic. Her love and respect is very tangible. Mirjam is a fine writer. We wrote a book together in German, *Love Inspires*, to explain to the people and the government the basic concept of how we work. The amount of bureaucracy from time to time did affect her enthusiasm. It made me feel helpless, as I was not able to help or to support her with this work because I was not used to the legal language. Christina, one of our sweet residents, would lift our spirits with her singing and dancing. Heike, Theresa and Carmen support Mirjam. Mirjam has handled bureaucracy and the transition very well. Even today she does it and secures our homes from legal and bureaucratic catastrophes. We are grateful to Mirjam and her talent.

*

By 2017 we had been running our homes successfully for twenty-seven years. I remember, as Heike, Mirjam and I were busy with the evaluation, a medical emergency occurred with one of our residents. We were sitting in our big winter garden.

Antje, a very competent and discreet caregiver, came to us. She announced there was an emergency with one of our old residents. We requested a break to deal with the emergency. With the help of another caregiver, Antje had prepared all that was needed according to the procedures. She had also ordered an ambulance. She just wanted to inform us.

Our emergency procedures reflect our attitude and care towards our residents. The love and care we offer spontaneously provide space and calm to residents. There is no panic, no stress. Despite emergencies, we move like a well-greased machine. The ambulance arrived and they took the resident. We went back to our evaluation and continued from where we had left off. This short break had demonstrated well where our priority lies. Our residents are at the centre of all that we do.

At lunch break, the examiner complimented the team, my management and our trust in the team that they could handle this emergency with ease and without going into a panic. The system for emergency response is foolproof. I explained to the examiner that in an emergency one needs absolute clarity of mind. In an emergency, one needs alertness and awareness and that is what we brought to the table.

*

In 2012, we had our second evaluation. This time it was a disaster. I felt that the examiners had already judged us and our concept in the light of my past. Each and every strong quality of the institute was viewed negatively.

For example, we have a stable workforce. Our average worker has been with us for fifteen years. This too was viewed negatively. They missed the point that a stable team provides a sense of security to the residents. To have this kind of stable team also means that the workers are satisfied with their management and the work atmosphere. No member of the team has even experienced a burnout in the thirty years we have been working.

The examiners spent two full days with us. They tried to find problems where there were none. They had a rude and arrogant attitude towards us and our residents. They made the residents uncomfortable. It brought tears to one of our residents who just wanted to offer a friendly greeting to them. The examiners forgot that the residents need acceptance and not rejection. Applying their prejudiced stereotypical idea of me, they accused me of not showing interest in the religion of my residents.

We exercise absolute freedom of religion in our homes. People are free to talk about their religious feelings if they want to. We do not engage the residents one way or another. We offer understanding and respect towards our residents and their religious feelings. We have the same approach towards our team too. We offer special diets according to the religious beliefs of the residents and the team. We celebrate various religious festivals too.

The examiners demanded that we be punctual. On both days, however, they came late. They tried to create stress among our team and unrest among the residents. After the examination was complete, they wrote a twenty-eight-page negative report about the institute. It was obvious that they wanted to show us in a bad light.

When Mirjam read the report, she burst out in disappointment. She felt violated. The evaluator's interpretations were far from the truth. She told me we could not accept this report. It was clear we had to seek legal help. She insisted, 'The report is not truthful, not just, and completely unfair. This report is against you personally, Sheela. You have worked hard in creating these homes.'

Heike, Mirjam and I read it again. It was clear that we could not accept the report. It violated our sense of responsibility towards our homes and our residents. We would have failed them by agreeing to such interpretations of our reality.

We tried to explain to the board of directors that we were victims of discrimination. We gave a number of examples to substantiate our claims. They refused to support us, saying that I was too sensitive because of my past. They declared they saw no reason to reject the report. The tone they used to declare the acceptance of the report was strange. Previously, our board never exerted such authority. They trusted us. They had always been well-wishers of the homes and my team. The board had direct contact with our residents. They knew the residents on a first-name basis and communicated with them openly. They were supporters of our work and concept. The board visited us every few weeks.

Now, this sudden change in them was curious. We could not understand. We thought of many excuses to dismiss our doubts, but I could not ignore a disturbing, uncertain feeling that something was wrong. We tried to ignore these feelings without success. I believed in my intuition. The mystery soon came to light. We found out that the board had organized a meeting with the Canton without our knowledge. This was not normal.

Mirjam, Heike and I decided to follow our feelings and move forward in protecting our homes. We looked for legal advice on the matter.

Soon we found a senior expert, a federal judge, in Basel. The advice he gave reflected his experience with law and the legal system. He gave his verdict. One could and should proceed with legal action. Mirjam and I felt vindicated. Our feeling was proven correct.

The board decided against legal action. We informed the members of the foundation of the situation. The members decided to get a new board. The board threatened to let me go by setting Heike and Mirjam against me. It did not work. Heike and Mirjam showed the most worthy quality of loyalty and declared, 'We see how Sheela works. Her dedication for her homes cannot be ignored.'

After this, we became aware of the danger to our institution. The future of our residents was of utmost importance to us. We could not walk away from it. The new board of directors agreed with us and decided to approach the government on this issue, and to support us with legal action if we could not resolve the problems amicably. It was a question of our existence and the well-being of our patients.

The new board felt like a gift from Existence. Today it feels like a reward for the work we do and have done. With this new board of directors, we feel safe and secure. The president of our foundation is a legal expert who worked as a Canton's judge for many years and also has a private legal practice. He mediated the differences between us and the Canton with the help of Mr Fair. He addressed our fears. Our evaluation was declared null and void.

Meanwhile, we hired experts who could help us with the implementation of the new law. We now understand that our examiners were not in compliance with the Regulation of Swiss Standards and Quality of Evaluation and also that their approach of evaluation did not follow the Quality Standards of Evaluation.

Rule 14

Be adventurous

It was in my childhood I learned the importance of travel. My father felt that through it, one could learn with much ease and fun about geography, people and tradition. And, it just happened to be that my work also encouraged travelling around the world.

After I started my homes in Switzerland, I began to miss my travels. I was also tied down in the country because of my legal situation. But since I wanted to integrate into Switzerland as quickly as I could, I soon started arranging short-distance outings with my old ladies. We all loved those trips. My ladies merrily sang Basel folk songs on the car drive.

One of the ninety-five-year-old residents of one of my homes had not left her village for years. So, I planned a week-long trip to Grindelwald and the Berner Oberland, about two-and-a-half hours from our house. This ninety-five-year-old woman had never imagined she would get to see the destination of her honeymoon ever again. She was deeply touched. Over coffee and cake, she told us the stories of her wedding and the honeymoon. The memories made her smile and lit up her face. It gave me an idea of the simplicity of their life when they were young. Listening to her, I felt my parents' absence acutely. My parents' needs and demands were little; they were easily content.

One of the eighty-year-old women in the homes was a midwife. She spoke about how she used to ski around in the middle of the night during the winter to deliver babies. Our postman, we found out, had come into the world through her competent delivery.

Soon, the excursions, from daily shopping to weeklong trips, became popular among my residents and their families. We began to undertake these experiences in 1992. We travelled to Graubünden, Appenzell and several other places in Switzerland. Our residents enjoyed the trips and benefited from them. Until then, psychologically, they had felt too weak to travel.

Trips, however, meant extra work. But that did not scare me. I became creative with the organization of these travels. First, I started with a small group of five people. Later, I successfully planned one for a bigger group of around thirty-eight people. We have travelled to distant parts of the world together as a group—Kenya, Egypt, Tenerife, Bulgaria, Croatia, Thailand, Bali, Vietnam, Greece, Turkey, Mauritius and Sri Lanka, among other places.

My residents cherish travelling. It brings them a sense of normalcy and builds deep trust within the group. Often, they learn to look after one another and start coming out of their shells. Their confidence in me and my team has increased manifold after such trips. In turn, this trust reduces their fears, lowers anxiety and improves their quality of life.

I organize these trips keeping in mind our safety, comfort and desires. I do not book cheap airlines to save money and the priority is clean and friendly hotels. To ensure safety, we make sure that our walk-away dementia residents are secure within the group. At night too, a caregiver will make sure to share a room with them. We speak to the hotel security to make sure extra attention is provided to those with orientation problems. Similarly, we inform the bars and restaurants not to serve alcohol to our group. We are always welcomed and received with pleasure in hotels around the world. We also get compliments from the other guests, who are often amazed by the behaviour of our group.

I, on my part, make sure to be there with the travelling group. During the trips, we often go out dancing in a disco or to eat, just anything that the residents can enjoy. I see to it that all activities organized are around food. They look forward to food during these fun breaks.

Our travel programme is a part of our official activities. Sometimes, I have to go away on business trips, only for short periods, but when I get back, the residents are always happy to see me. The homecoming is so warm that it makes me feel as if I was gone for much longer than I really was.

Rule 15

Love enough so you can let go

As I write this, I feel as if I am reliving a very important event from my past. Back then, I was at a crossroads of emotions. I had to make a choice; I had to perform the highest duty of love, one that I felt for Cora, my dog.

I had inherited Cora twelve-and-a-half years ago from one of my octogenarian patients, Mary. She had two children, a daughter and a son. Both were psychologically challenged. The son, Paul, had been a resident in Matrusaden Residence in Switzerland for about twelve years; he was stabilized and doing well.

It was one morning in 2006 that I had received a call from a social worker, Mrs S, from a nearby town. She needed an emergency bed for Mary, Paul's mother. Finding a placement for Mary at a home was proving to be difficult for her. She had contacted most of the old age homes in the state but had no success.

The problem, it appeared, was that she had a dog. Mary had refused to give the dog away to an animal shelter and most homes did not accept pets. To add to the problem, the dog barked constantly.

The social worker remarked, 'You have a dog in your home. I figured you might accept Mary and the dog.' She continued without giving me a chance to say anything, 'If not, I will have to forcefully take her dog to a shelter. Mary needs care; she is not well psychologically or physically to look after both herself and the dog. The neighbours are complaining about her dog barking day and night. You are my last hope!'

I react well to difficult situations and here I was faced with another one. I can think fast and clear in an emergency but Mrs S talked desperately, rarely giving me a chance to get in a word. I interrupted her when she paused to take a breath and asked, 'Can I see Mary? When can I see her? Can I also meet her dog?'

She replied, 'Can you come now? I am with Mary at her apartment. It is an emergency.'

I could sense the urgency in her tone.

I know myself. I could never leave Mary in the cold, especially when she needed my help. It is just not in my nature to walk away or shy away from sticky situations. I took the address and told her I would be there in thirty minutes.

I took Heike and Mirjam, my two trusted lieutenants, along with me and we drove to Mary's apartment. Mrs S was eagerly waiting for us in the parking lot of the building. She explained quickly that she had a directive from her superior to resolve the issue the same day. The neighbours had been complaining and they wanted to avoid legal problems.

As soon as we entered the apartment, it all became clear to me. The rooms were filthy and unhygienic. It was obvious that the dog had not been taken out for walks for days. In fact, I spotted its droppings in places. The dog was continuously barking and Mary was lying on a dirty bed. It was not a pleasant sight and it made sense why Mrs S was desperate to evacuate Mary and the dog without any delay.

I didn't have to think, I had to help! Yet again the Universe had provided an opportunity to be creative. I said to Mrs S, 'I will take them both for now, if Mary allows me, and do my best to stabilize them. But what should I do if Cora has trouble adjusting with my dog or ends up biting the residents?'

Mrs S relaxed a bit and said, 'You can put the dog in a shelter or give it to someone. Take any decision you want. I will talk to the shelter so that you can bring the dog as per your discretion.'

My secretaries Heike and Mirjam know me well. At that moment back then, they were shocked but they expected me to agree. When I am in doubt, I always say yes and remain positive. So, they did not ask questions and started packing Mary's clean clothes and medicines. We left the rest of her belongings. It was Mrs S's responsibility to wind up and return the keys to the apartment to the owner.

Heike, Mirjam and I left with Mary and the dog for Matrusaden. Mary was happy to learn that she was going to be living near her son Paul.

Soon our nurses took charge of Mary while I took care of Cora. She was a beautiful dog. We played the 'My Fair Lady' routine which involved her showering and grooming. It also involved walks, but it was painful to watch her body language for she walked hugging the garden wall with her tail between the legs. She was afraid and insecure and therefore at the same time, alert and watchful.

We prepared a bed for Cora and to our delight, my dog Raja, accepted young Cora willingly. Raja was old and it seemed that he missed his sister Lalli, who had died about four months ago. He was kind and allowed Cora to be a part of the household graciously.

It was important for me to watch and observe Mary, Cora and Raja closely. We aimed to make them comfortable and create a sense of trust so that they could quickly begin feeling at home.

For the first few days, Mary proved to be difficult to manage. She would hold Cora by her collar and trouble her by pulling her about. This did not help Cora's insecurities—no wonder she barked a lot. We felt that it was important to move Cora away from Mary. To our dismay, Mary was not ready to do that. We had to be very tactful and so, one morning when Mary was in the shower, we moved Cora's bed under my desk. Within three days, Cora grew comfortable there and started to feel secure. Mary tried to take her out of there by pulling on her collar, but I stopped her and tried to explain to her that this was where Cora would sleep. Cora had to have the freedom of movement and could not be held captive.

It was a bitter pill to swallow for Mary. She cried a bit and wanted to return to her apartment, but after three days, she accepted the new reality.

Meanwhile, Cora slowly began to calm down in the hygienic environment and even enjoyed the dog food we fed her. It took about a couple of months, but Cora started enjoying her walks. She was soon running in the fields. Her body language also changed slowly. She felt secure. It was around this time that Mary suffered a heart attack and passed away.

It was heartbreaking, however, when Mary's daughter Jennet came to claim the inheritance. Jennet wanted to take Cora away. The residents and my team all pleaded that I do not give up Cora. I too did not want her to leave. According to the law, however, Cora was Mary's possession; I had to comply. But I told Jennet, 'If you feel you cannot handle her or if she proves to be troublesome for you, simply call me. I will come and pick her up.'

Since Jennet lived in a small apartment, I even tried telling her that Cora could be difficult. But my efforts were all in vain. I had to reluctantly give her up.

We were sad to see Cora go and waited for the telephone call. The entire day, we repeatedly looked out at the parking lot hoping Cora would somehow run back home. I waited in the night, went out of the house a couple of times and checked the parking lot to see if she had returned. But nothing. The next morning, we wanted to know how she was doing. Heike decided to phone Jennet. Jennet informed Heike that Cora was happy and doing well. We knew Cora and therefore had a hard time believing it, but we had no option other than to accept Jennet's words. That morning was quite sad for all of us. Deep inside though, we hoped for the phone to ring. By lunch, there was no news. At the lunch table, we started talking about Cora. I put on a brave face and reminded us, 'Guys, we have to accept it and wish Cora all the best.'

Just then, the telephone rang. Mirjam and Heike both jumped and ran towards the phone, desperately hoping it was regarding Cora. And sure enough, it was a distraught Jennet on the phone. Heike passed the phone to me.

'Can you take Cora back? I cannot have two dogs in the apartment,' Jennet said.

I remained cool in my response. I did not want Jennet to change her mind because of my excitement. I assured Jennet that I fully understood her position. I wanted her to tell me the time and address, so I could pick Cora up. I know I would have gone to the moon if required. But Jennet continued talking, without a word on her location.

I interrupted her impatiently and asked, 'Can you give me the address for where I should meet you?'

'SBB railway station, Basel,' she responded.

I simply told her, 'I will be there in 30 minutes.'

Euphoric, I immediately left with Mirjam for SBB. Lunch was not important that day and we could not drive fast enough.

We quickly spotted them on a footpath outside SBB, Basel. We ran to Cora. I took Cora in my arms, kissed her sweet nose many times and hugged her. She was excited to see me. We let Cora know that we were there to take her back home. Then, I turned my attention to Jennet.

Jennet did not want to talk much about what had happened or why she had chosen to return Cora. I was not interested either; I was happy to just have Cora back. Jennet bid us goodbye and left quickly. That was when Mirjam and I both noticed that Cora was petrified. She was shivering, her eyes searched for danger! We took her to the car and tried to calm her down by petting, kissing and talking with her. It took us a while before she stopped shivering and started breathing normally.

We came home to a celebration, akin to the sort provided to war veterans returning from a battle. Our team and residents were eagerly waiting for us. As we opened the car door, Cora ran into the house. She greeted everyone and went under my desk; she was at home.

I took official responsibility for Cora. She became my daughter—Cora Birnstiel! In my eyes, she could do no wrong. She became the princess of the home. She took on the royal responsibility of protecting us and keeping us all very happy. It seems she performed her duties too well. Whenever an outsider visited or when she heard a car or a stranger entering, she would bark. She even protected residents when they went for their daily walks. She would sit around us, staying watchful to protect us.

She was the medicine no pharmaceutical company has for dementia. She understood it intuitively and even Alzheimer without any training. She knew exactly how to approach the residents and lick their hands or feet or sit by them.

She was aware of her own trauma from her youth and remained true to herself and the reality with gratitude. When her life became better, she did not take it for granted. At the same time, she was not bitter about her sad childhood. She moved on and took charge of the remainder of her life. She was a true daughter, teacher and a friend to me—she was my inspiration.

* * *

Death and departure have been a big part of my life. It is a reality that we all must deal with. Eventually, the time came to say goodbye to Cora. She was fourteen years old when she left us. In her final year, she developed a tumour on her neck. The tumour was the size of a melon. We considered getting it operated on, but her doctor advised against it. I did not want her to suffer. As long as she had an interest in living, in the environment around her and she was not in pain, I was happy to support her in her fight with the tumour.

However, I had an arrangement with the doctor—that as and when I felt that she had pain or difficulty in breathing—I would bring Cora to him to put her to sleep. And these were the instructions to my team as well for the time wasn't there. They were all in agreement. I wanted Cora to be cremated and for her ashes to be dispersed in the house garden near the samadhi of my parents, my two other dogs, Lalli and Raja and my rabbits.

Cora could sense that the day of her departure was very near as she was becoming weaker each passing day. She had lost over 10 kg in the last six months. She also slept a lot. Despite that, she continued to go on walks with the residents. She did not run as much as she used to. We did not force her into any activities. She was exempted from all rules. Her wish was our command.

During those days I would talk with Cora daily, tell her that her time with us was limited. I would thank her for her love and care for me and the commune. She would look at me with sad eyes. Her sadness stemmed from the idea of ultimate separation, from departing this loving life. I felt as if she understood every word I said, that she responded by licking my face or hand, saying that she felt the same.

It had become routine for Cora to sit by the dinner table while we were eating. I would share my food with her by feeding her small bites. When I was finished, I would pick up my iPad and iPhone and go to my room. This little routine with Cora was the highlight of the day for both of us. It was the perfect way to end a good, productive day. This was our time together, along with when I would return from my travels. All dog experts say not to feed dogs at a table and spoil them; I never understood why.

I, of course, am in no position to critique dog experts as I never felt that Cora was anything but my daughter. Nor was I stupid enough to give up these rich, profound events of my life.

Cora possessed the same qualities and madness that I had. She cared for us the way I cared for her and the others. As her tumour grew, Cora's hind legs became weak. At times she needed help to climb up the stairs. Still, she managed to somehow go to my room on the first floor of the house in the evenings. I saw and felt her difficulty. It broke my heart each time.

On 28 August 2018, I decided to not ask Cora to go upstairs. After my dinner, I went to my desk to pick up my iPad and iPhone and say goodnight to her. But Cora was not under the desk. She was not in the winter garden or the parking lot either.

We all got very concerned. I ran up to see if she was on the bed. She had earlier tried to go up to the room, but she was unable to climb more than three steps. She could not possibly be on the bed, I thought, as I ran up.

And sure enough, there she was, on the bed, waiting for me. We spent a few minutes talking to each other about life and death. The high point of life is the moment of death. We both knew we could not avoid separation. However, saying the final goodbye is never easy. We both needed strength to face the situation.

The next day, on 29 August, Cora knew it was her last day. She saw tears in my eyes; I spotted the same in hers. All residents and the team sang and bid her goodbye. We prepared Cora a nice comfortable bed in the car. Heike and I took her to the doctor. We stayed with her till the very end. She felt our fingers and tears on her body until her last breath. She was surrounded by our love in her final journey. Cora is gone, but her love and loyalty remain with us in our hearts and memory.

Rule 16

Live in the moment; be positive and make the most of what you have without any expectations

We call the room for the residents' intense care the 'Demenz Mandir' or the temple of dementia. It is a pilot project born out of great concern for our dementia residents— those who are very sick and at the end of their journeys. In Swiss homes for those with severe disabilities, you will not find such living options. We were granted permission to start this project and it has proven to be very successful; it is truly a 'mandir'.

The Demenz Mandir is in our living room, at the entrance of our house. This allows the dementia residents to hear the music, telephone, laughter and individuals entering and leaving. They see and feel life in full movement. The Demenz Mandir is a loving, special place for my residents. They are occupied with the daily noise and activity around them. We have some of our office desks in the same room. This way, a part of the team is constantly near them. We do this because, in the last moments of life, it is important that they are surrounded by warmth and care.

This concept of Demenz Mandir proved to be evolutionary in our home. We have three floors. All bedrooms are on the first and second floor. In the beginning, we had all our residents, including dementia residents, sleeping upstairs. During the day, after their showers, we brought them downstairs, where they remained for the rest of the day. This worked well for a while.

But soon, I had three residents who required special care. I did not feel comfortable leaving them on their beds alone during the day as they needed their special hospital beds.

After a while, I noticed that being alone frightened them; they would become insecure and restless. I was certain they needed to be near us, between us, where the activity was, someplace they would not feel alone. They understood feelings, but were oblivious to the words and norms of the social order. They reacted to music, laughter and smiles positively. They felt the warmth of touch.

The next day I moved our dining table into our living room, therefore creating space for beds for my heavy-care residents. It worked out very well. Their beds upstairs remained available to them in case they wanted to sleep upstairs. I felt secure that they were under my wing. The situation had an added advantage. The younger residents started developing an interest in the heavy-care residents. A natural integration of the two groups started to take place. It allowed the old residents to feel young, while the young learned of old age, which in turn, alleviated their fear of what was to come.

Dementia is helplessness and sadness. Many old people suffer from it. However, nowadays even some of the young struggle with it as it can be brought upon by alcohol and drug addiction. I have dealt with several such cases.

I remember a sixty-year-old man who had paid us a visit with his son. He was accomplished and had invented an important medication. They were looking for a secure place where the father could move in. As I have shared, our home is open to all.

At the early age of sixty, he had been diagnosed with Alzheimer's disease and dementia. He spoke nine languages despite his health conditions. But he had lost his grip on life. Because he could speak well, people assumed he was normal. No one could tell that he had an illness. Speaking fluently can be so deceiving.

The man could not sit still. He was always on the go. He would walk away, get on the train and travel to the final station, for he had no fixed destination. He did not know where to go and when to return. He was lost mentally. This constant need to run away made it difficult for his family. They would have trouble tracking him. And more importantly, his family was busy leading their own lives. They had no idea how to contain the man during the day, how to help or deal with someone who had lost his faculties.

It was also difficult for many to try and understand that a man of his education and achievements could need the supervision required for a child. His invention had helped many around the world and continued to do so. But fate had diagnosed him with Alzheimer's disease.

I have experienced that dementia can make one forget what has been learned, but it does not affect one's nature. Dementia patients understand feelings, touch and sound. They are attracted to positivity. Negativity frightens them. They enjoy human warmth intuitively.

I often ask myself questions about life. What do education and money mean?

Somehow, I always arrive at this: Live in the moment. Be positive and make the most of what you have without any expectations.

I try my best to follow this. It works. It makes life easier and the futility of it does not get me down. I use these teachings daily with my dementia residents. I manage my expectations.

I am not charmed or amused by their achievements or languages. I am simply happy if they smile or tap their feet to music or sleep without any fear. For me, that is enough.

I have also noticed that individuals with dementia feel, in the beginning, that something in their life has changed. They feel confused and their lack of understanding causes fear. They lose their sense of time. They feel like a ship in a storm, without an anchor.

That is why when they are among other people, they feel secure and comfortable. If they are left alone at home, they will forget to turn off their stove or leave the water running in their kitchens or bathrooms. This can prove to be dangerous to them and others.

This behaviour is not deliberate. In the beginning, one might think it is done to annoy, but no, it is simply that they have lost the ability to think. Please do not be quick to judge or blame. Have sympathy and understanding. Be patient. They should be cared for in all situations, day and night.

This reminds me of an incident with a ninety-year-old resident. It was a cold winter morning with a bit of snow outside. I was busy helping another resident to the shower. My team and I were busy with daily routine work. We had closed our main door without locking it. We only lock the doors at night. We did not think anyone would walk out.

I was ready to shower Mrs M.M. I had last left her in the dining room with a cup of coffee. She was a dementia patient. When I returned, she was nowhere to be seen. I looked around, in her room, kitchen and in other rooms. One of the residents told me she went out through the main door. I could not believe it.

She was ninety years old, small built, with little strength in her arms to open our heavy main door. I wondered how she did it.

However, that was not the time to try and figure that out. It was an emergency because it was snowing and she was wearing only her bathrobe and house sandals. I figured she must be cold. Not to mention, she could have slipped on the frozen road.

With individual cars, two of us went to search for her. Another team member ran to search the side of the road.

We figured that she could not have gone too far. But we came home without her after fifteen minutes. I decided to call the police for help and went to my office desk for the telephone.

My office desk overlooks our small garden and I have this beautiful view of Sonnenberg. In the corner of the garden was a thirty-metre-high pine tree. With the phone to my ear, I saw something colourful hanging on the tree. I moved to see what it was.

I burst out laughing. It was funny and I was overjoyed to see what it was. I instantly hung up the phone and called my team to enjoy the sight.

It was Mrs M.M. sitting on the tree, three metres high.

We never understood how she managed to climb the tree in her bathrobe or how she opened the heavy main door. Once we got her down from the tree, we warmed her up with a hot drink and thick clothes. She laughed with us and it truly felt like a miraculous moment.

It was a big lesson for my team and me to never underestimate dementia of any kind.

If you judge or expect certain behaviour from dementia patients, you will be disappointed. This disappointment may lead to anger. And anger is the opposite of what it requires. Dementia's prescription is positivity and gentle handling. This sacred positivity in me and my team is what has created the concept of Demenz Mandir. It works well and we receive lots of compliments for it. Most importantly, our residents feel happy and comfortable. They live a life free of anxiety.

Transitioning to death is not easy. One needs much discretion while working with people. Despite the inevitability of death, most people fear it. They are uncomfortable talking about it. Death is unknown territory. At the same time, it is the only thing one can be certain of. It is tabooed. It has been pushed into the back corners. The fear of death is natural and the culmination of all our lives. In experiencing and acknowledging this, we reduce its power over us.

In our homes, most of the residents (and the team) fear death. While it is certain that everyone will die one day, it is the date that one does not know. So, when such fear is displayed, which occurs almost daily, we explain to our residents individually the futility of the fear. Our non-taboo approach to death makes it easier to deal with the topic.

We make jokes about it and make light of this heavy subject. This does not bring results immediately, but it slowly wears off the fear and in time, our residents learn to laugh about it. Thereby, this theme becomes less prominent in daily life for them.

One has to be free of one's mundane burdens of life. At the end of one's life, one has to be content. This contentment is the result of acceptance of life that one has lived without judgment and with gratefulness.

Life is often easier than the last moment of death. I have cared for a number of dying residents. The smell of death would surround them, but they would suffer for days and weeks. Their problem was that they had unfinished, unfulfilled situations in their life, which they could not resolve. Often such situations are family-related. I try and tell them to speak to their families, help them understand how important it is to work out these conflicts. The idea is to approach residents on their deathbed with positive forgiving energy, so that they can find the same energy within themselves and let go of the conflict.

This positivity helps them relax as they approach the end of their life. They are able to let go of their bodies peacefully and fly free from this world. I also see to it that we try to accommodate their small wishes. I know how important it is that one leaves this world content of all wishes.

I feel that each person has the right to decide to pull the plug on themselves. And if they have lost the ability to decide for themselves then they should trust their families and doctors to do so. It has been my experience that death needs no one's permission. Death comes when the person is ready from within. The moment emotional ties are unlocked, death arrives. It comes when one is alone. Therefore all wise men talk of detachment and being free from worldly emotions and possessions. They are the bondages. They will keep you from your bodily freedom at the time of death.

Our terminal residents, like others, are showered and changed into fresh clothes every day. Their beds are cleaned daily. We wash their mouths with refreshing moisturizing lemon and glycerine swabs. We talk to them and let them feel that we are near them, with our smiles and touch. Every one of us goes to them and lets them feel that we are there for them and that there is nothing to worry about. In our home, we treat the entire process of death and dying with sacred respect. We are aware of the importance of this last, highest moment of life. It cannot be missed by anyone. After the doctor's visit, we give them the last wash. We all gather to say our last goodbyes to them. There is nothing morbid or dark in our approach.

I have seen death from a young age as I've lost a number of loved ones to terminal illnesses. But after spending time with my father, mother and Bhagwan, the fear of death soon dissipated. When one lives around loved ones, sorrow and regrets soon disappear. Otherwise, death cuts short the wishes of life. I have lived a very intense and full life in every situation.

I have no reason to fear death. For myself, I would like a natural death as and when it comes. I would not like to medically prolong my life. At the same time, unless I am suffering from excessive pain day in and day out, I do not need help from an organization such as 'Exit' (institute for help with death). I feel that I will have enough courage and strength to accept it graciously, without being greedy for more time. I live my life so fully and intensely that more years are not required. I want to accept death just as I have accepted life. I have seen my mother and father die graciously. I want to go the same way.

* * *

Many a time, I have seen people's bodies dearly hanging on in the final moments. But the resolution does not arrive until one has found peace from all emotions. This happened to one of my residents.

An old woman lived the last few years of her life in my home. She was suffering from Alzheimer's. She spoke no English or German and yet I had a wonderful relationship with her. She understood feelings and conveyed her likes and dislikes through her smile, frown or wordless sounds. She was not in a condition to be alone. Her daughter had brought her to us. She did not want her mother living alone or at their house when she would go out for work. It was a good solution as she wanted her to be nearby.

The mother and daughter shared a good relationship. The daughter was always there for her when needed and I never felt that the mother was a burden for her. Despite that, there were unresolved feelings between the two of them. These were old unresolved feelings from her childhood and youth.

We are all victims of such unnecessary feelings of misunderstandings. We all carry excess baggage of feelings throughout our life. Many ruin their lives because of such events and become bitter. Many do not have the understanding or a generous heart to resolve such feelings and unburden themselves from such unwanted negativity. What we often forget is how important it is to simply have a big heart, to forgive and forget. At the time of death, such conflicts and bitterness become transparent.

While the mother was ready to die, this unresolved feeling between daughter and mother would not allow her to go in peace. There was unfinished business. The daughter was heartbroken. She did not know how to work out this conflict with her mother. The daughter wanted her mother to leave the world in peace. She wanted to forgive and forget the conflict, but the mother had Alzheimer's. She thought that her illness would prevent her from understanding her feelings.

I felt her dilemma. In four years of her mother's stay with me, we had developed a good friendship. She opened her heart to me. She cried. She asked me, 'Sheela, what can I do? It is too late!'

I told her, 'It is not late at all. It is the right time now. Her mind is not there, but her heart and feelings are very much present. Now you must find a way to communicate to her.'

She cried, 'How?'

'It is simple. You hold her hands, stroke her head and kiss her. She would feel it. She knows you from when you were in her womb. She will understand. On your part, be generous. Do not expect that your mother will spring up and kiss you and beg your forgiveness. Remain open and the wounds will heal. Wounds do heal. I am confident,' I said.

She remained all afternoon at her mother's side. She held her mother's hands and bringing them to her lips, kissed them gently. Tears rolled down without restrain. These tears washed the infected wounds of many years. From the mother's closed sleepy eyes, tears dropped on the pillow.

The storm of emotion started to settle. There was a tangible serenity around the mother. Her face had relaxed. Some of the old deep lines of unhappiness were visibly gone. The daughter too felt lighter in her heart.

The daughter came to me at my work desk. It was only three metres away from her mother's bed. Our nursing station for very sick and dying residents is also in the same area. She took me in her arms and hugged me tightly. Tears were still rolling down her cheeks. She whispered emotionally, 'Thank you. Thank you for helping me resolve this lifetime problem with my mother. Now I am free of it. I feel light. But I cannot stop crying.'

I replied, 'Cry till the tears dry out by themselves. It will wash your heart.'

These three hours of communication between the mother and daughter had healed all wounds of the past. The next morning, the mother died in peace. For me, it was a miracle.

One is sad to lose a loved one, but the sadness does not shadow the rest of one's life when the feelings are resolved and one is free of the emotional burden. This freedom is important for the living and the dead.

Rule 17

Make new mistakes every day instead of repeating the same mistakes

A lot of people in the world do not get the opportunity to learn new ways of thinking. They don't get to travel enough to experience other cultures and traditions. I have always believed that to learn and come out of one's cocoon, one must take risks in life. This understanding was offered to me and my siblings by our parents when we were young.

I try to offer this exposure to my team in whatever way I can. Being in the public eye, we have many visitors from around the world. After their visits, I talk to my team about the experiences I have undergone throughout the course of my life. I try to ease their fears of the unknown and encourage them to be bold and expressive. I remind them not to be afraid of expressing their emotions; it is not a sign of weakness, it reflects your honesty and your emotional vulnerability. Often this bold expression of emotions rubs off on others, making them sympathetic.

I want my team to be satisfied with the work environment we have created. I want them to know and feel that they are important to me. Without them, I cannot carry out my work and I do not shy away from expressing my feelings with them.

The truth is that my book will be incomplete if I don't talk about them.

For me, my team is the same as my residents. We are interwoven through the moments of emotional joy, stress or crisis we have shared. I have a dedicated team of twenty-seven people with diverse skills and personalities. Our household experts complement our nursing staff. Our young kitchen workers support our caregivers in caring for our residents. Our office staff help everyone with writing reports and assist the rest of the staff with feeding our dementia patients or in an emergency, even cleaning dishes, making breakfast or giving baths to the patients.

The first principle of our team is that we are equals and we are here to help our residents and support one another. This creates a relaxed atmosphere and fosters team spirit. Stress has no place in our lives and homes.

My main work is to train the team and provide an overview of each function, system and routine. When I do that, I keep each person's qualities and weaknesses in mind. Our work schedule reflects the strength of our collective qualities.

Some of our team members are perceptive and quick learners and are eager to take up more responsibilities. As far as I am concerned, the responsibilities are ready to be taken! It is a gesture my team and I appreciate.

We provide individual guidance to all team members. I encourage the team to interact among themselves without passing undue judgement or engaging in gossip. This forms the second principle of our team.

The third and most important principle is proper planning. The work schedule is prepared meticulously and in a manner that is fair to my whole team. When we prepare the schedule, we make sure both houses are covered with enough caretakers, kitchen staff, secretaries for meetings and guardians for the residents. We ensure that psychiatric meetings, doctor's and dentist's visits are planned and carried out efficiently. Additionally, we make proper arrangements for the management of correspondence, telephones and office documentation plus emergency cover. We also employ a housemaster to maintain two beautiful houses in good condition.

Instead of split shifts, I prefer my team to work two-hour shifts that are longer, but allow the team to have more personal or family time. Our home is open to all and that includes children and pets. Children benefit from being close to their parents at all times. In turn, the parents are put at ease by the knowledge that their child is surrounded by co-workers, residents and other children, instead of spending time alone at home. The presence of children running and playing invigorates the residents; it makes them feel as if they are a part of a community, a family. These small considerations motivate my team and in turn, my team can assist me as I assist them, in my times of crises.

Our tasks far exceed the time we need to finish them. On some days, despite our efforts, my team of twenty-seven is also not enough. It gets difficult to prepare the work schedule during school vacation times, for I need to consider the situation of workers with children and coordinate their off-days with those of their children. However, some senior members put the priorities of the institution above their personal needs and I am ever grateful for those solid pillars of our team who are always ready to support us.

Our care homes provide our residents with a safe and reliable environment. Our reliability is the result of a stable and well-trained team. My team is a reflection of who I am; I do not expect them to do anything that I am not ready to do myself. Whatever I have learned, I pass on to them.

Our residents and team members come from a wide variety of cultural backgrounds. At the moment, we have people from fifteen nationalities in our homes. It might sound unusual, but we do not have visiting hours. We are open for spontaneous visits from anyone at all times.

Regardless of their certifications, our members work side by side on all tasks. I discourage politics or power dynamics based on member's certifications. Carmen and Manuela are a part of our certified team and they received their certification while working with us. We offered them all the support they needed for the completion of their studies. Both have learned a lot on the job and have benefited by becoming familiar with the technical language used in our field of work. Carmen supports our office team and has proved herself to be an invaluable asset.

Manuela takes care of Bapusaden with two other experienced team members. She manages reports and filing to ensure that our homes comply with government guidelines.

Mirjam is well versed in the language of government documentation. She keeps us all fully informed about government rules and regulations, and her contribution to our existence is unique and immense.

What can I say about Shpresa? She has been my constant companion for the past twenty-one years. Her strong and gentle heart sets her apart as one of the most special members of my team. Dashuri is our silent and dependable worker. Her silence is her strength. Rebecca is our nurse, calm and poised for all emergencies. Medicine distribution is her responsibility and she does it very well.

There is a healthy interaction among our team members. After our residents have their meals, the team sits down to eat together. The act of sharing a meal and discussing the day's events and our personal lives, candidly and without the fear of judgement, brings us closer.

Team differences affect the residents adversely. They tend to pick up on intra-team conflicts intuitively and try to bend them to their advantage. This makes our work burdensome and complicated. My colleagues know that I don't like to play the blame game. I know that there is no room for excuses. I have learned the importance of taking responsibility for my actions and mistakes from my parents and Bhagwan.

My mother used to say: 'When you point a finger at someone remember three fingers are pointing at you . . .'

No one gets punished or even fired for making mistakes. Instead, I make sure to help my team resolve those mistakes. As my father used to say, 'Every mistake can be a stepping stone for a new understanding.' My mantra for my team is: make new mistakes every day instead of repeating the same mistakes.

I remember a story Bhagwan told me once.

'Seela, how can you tell the difference between man and animal?'

'It is simple,' Bhagwan answered. 'Animals don't repeat their mistakes.'

Bhagwan explained a profound lesson in simple words to me and I have always kept it in mind.

Eventually, for our homes to function smoothly, the team has to learn to complement one another. They have to work as a single unit. A sense of unity will ensure that the work environment is stress-free and pleasant, that the work itself doesn't feel repetitive and that the workers have the energy to enjoy their free time after the day's work is done.

I am again reminded of a story Bhagwan told me about Lao-Tse.

Lao-Tse was a judge in his village.

He had to pass judgment on a legal case between a thief and a rich man.

Lao-Tse asks the thief, 'Is the claim of the rich man that you stole from him correct?'

'Yes, your honour, my family had nothing to eat for a few days . . .' replied the thief.

Lao-Tse explained to the thief that he had made a mistake and would have to be punished for it, as the law forbade stealing. 'You have my compassion for your hungry family.'

The rich man was happy with Lao-Tse's verdict and the punishment for the thief.

Lao-Tse turned towards the rich man and said, 'I have to give you a punishment as well. I do not find the thief alone in the wrongdoing. I find that you have also broken the law. You have hoarded many riches. Indirectly you are responsible for this poor man's family's condition and his act of theft. If you would not have collected all that you could and given him work, his family would have had enough to eat and he would not have had to steal . . .'

The observers and the rich man in the court were stunned by Lao-Tse's verdict. For me, Lao-Tse's fair judgement was absolute and praiseworthy.

Rule 18

Never forget your roots

At last, I have reached the end of my saga. I don't know if I will get an opportunity to write again or if I will be capable of it, as age presents its restrictions. I remain open to life, with all the surprises and opportunities it has to offer. I remain thankful to all who have helped me in my life's journey; I will continue to undertake it with gratitude in my heart.

Writing this book was not an easy task, for it was delayed by a year due to an accident with a forty-year-old resident suffering from dementia. This resident, though big and physically strong, had a rare illness. He had lost his speech and had a hard time walking. Whenever I got an opportunity, I would walk with him. Last year in June, one morning, I was walking with him in our parking lot.

I noticed he was having trouble walking and tried to assist him by holding him from the side, supporting him so he would remain upright. However, I could not hold him till help came. He was almost double my size. Finally, he could control himself no longer and I suffered a hard fall to the ground.

I ended up with two fractures on my vertebra. I was unable to sit for long and was in constant pain. Despite this, I tried to continue my work by lying on the sofa in our Demenz Mandir. My team was my biggest support during my recovery.

In those trying times, the determination and willpower I had built came to my rescue. I have treated all bodily illnesses with clarity and inner strength. I had seen my father go through severe illness without collapsing under bodily pain. I had exercised this determination with Bhagwan and with building his commune. No excuses are good enough, that is my inner understanding. I decided to continue to function despite the pain.

It was then I got an offer to write a book. I could not pass up this opportunity, being the eternal opportunist that I am. Yet another adventure, I thought. I did not commit myself entirely but promised to try and write. I started to write, but after a few pages, I had to stop, as I could not sit for more than a few short minutes at a time. My fractures were not healing fast enough. Three months had passed and yet my pain was excruciating. To put breaks on my activity was not on my agenda. But I had to. The doctors decided to operate on my back. I had no choice but to accept, against the wishes of all my loved ones.

I lost a whole year to the recovery process and I am still not completely pain-free. I continue to do physiotherapy and exercise regularly.

In 2019, I was invited to the Dehradun Literature Festival. I took this as a sign to write the book I had till then kept on hold. I kept my promise to my publisher to write and completed the book.

In these moments of contentment, I had thoughts of visiting India again before I disappeared from this world. I did not pursue these feelings actively as I did not want to upset my loved ones, especially my sisters Mira and Maya, with their imaginary worries. I did not know if that moment would ever arrive. Would I be left waiting forever? I knew clearly that if Existence wished it, it would happen and no one would be able to stop it. In March 2019, Anurag Chauhan sent me an email inviting me to India. I could not refuse. I felt an immediate 'Yes' rise up in me. However, I did not want to say yes before my sister Mira had given her consent. I also had my two secretaries' wishes to consider.

I called Mira, Mirjam and Heike together. I read them the email from Anurag. I asked them and told them that if they say 'No' then I will accept their decision. To my surprise, Mira said 'Yes, but with the condition that you take Heike and Mirjam with you . . .'

Just the thought of India provokes many emotions in me. I was going to visit my home country after thirty-four long years; I was curious to know how I would feel after spending so many years away. The feeling of nostalgia excited me; it was almost like being under my parents' wings again. Life was coming full circle for me. I lived almost seventeen years of my life in India. It was here that I experienced some of the most precious and formative moments of my life. It is time that I look back and reflect upon some of these.

Would I be objective or emotional? Would I remember bits and pieces of a long-forgotten childhood?

I felt elated that my sister and my team felt it was about time for me to visit India. I felt new energy rushing into my bones. I could hardly stop smiling. At night, I could not sleep with a storm of thoughts brewing in my head about my upcoming trip to India. Mira advised us to apply for the Indian Visa right away.

I was uncertain about obtaining the Visa successfully. I had no clue about the working of Indian politics or how my messy departure from Bhagwan was viewed in India! I reminded myself that if my trip was planned by Existence, then things will work out. I decided to quell my doubts and stay positive.

As luck would have it, logistically, it all worked out well. We experienced no setbacks in our trip. I had a number of conversations with Anurag; I expressed my doubts and concerns to him. He eased my worries with words of comfort and reassurance. One of my predominant worries was whether I would be able to deliver what was expected of me. This worry came as I had not been in touch with India for decades. This distance, of both time and space, had made me a stranger to my own home country.

Due to my hectic work schedule, I was able to overcome all excitement regarding our impending trip. Finally, it was the day I had been waiting for; on 26 September 2019 we arrived at the New Delhi International Airport. I looked forward to this new adventure. Anurag had arranged for someone to help us through immigration. I took in my surroundings with unabashed awe; the people, the smell of home, the rising tide of excitement, were making me feel as if I was having an out-of-body experience. I looked up and around to make sure I was on Earth. Somehow, I felt I was in the twilight zone. My expectations and disappointment vanished, replaced by the shocking yet comforting reality of finally being home. The smiling faces and noises I was not accustomed to, made me smile back. It was an unreal reality. Mirjam and Heike were in a daze; Heike was happy to forget a personal tragedy for a while and Mirjam obsessed over my safety. With the help of our guide, we came out of the arrival gate where Anurag and a few other people, who were part of the receiving team, surrounded us. It was then that I saw a camera team; I took it as normal. But Mirjam and Heike were not so sure! Their priority was to protect me.

We were soon confronted by our first crisis. I was rushed to a waiting car. Mirjam and Heike panicked! Mirjam had managed, with her elbows over the camera team, to find a place in the car. Heike however, could not. I made a quick decision and sent Heike, to the next car. I almost lost twenty years of friendship in a few short minutes!

As our car proceeded towards the hotel, the film crew started bombarding me with questions. We had not been made aware of our schedule, as prepared by the trip organizer, which threw us into uncertainty. After a short drive, we reached the hotel. A good night's sleep was what it took for things to start falling into place. My five and a half week's trip to India was interesting and fun. I had a tight schedule; our time was packed with speaking events, individual meetings and filming. A film crew tailed me like a shadow. Of course, my companions and I were not used to this. But we quickly adapted to it all. In preparation for these events, we had to be fitted with proper clothing. This was a new experience for me as I had never been to designers, though I had been acknowledged as a fashion icon. The whole experience was interesting, to say the least. When I would try outfits there, a number of well-wishers would accompany me. When I would step out of the changing room, there would be ten different interpretations of my attire. However, it was my privilege to make the final decision.

Once I was trying an outfit and the tailor's name was Bhagwan. It was music to my ears. I know that Bhagwan has since long passed away, but the familiar name brought cherished memories to the surface of my mind. I went to him and hugged him. We took a few photos with him. That day I thought to myself, 'Bhagwan can truly come in many forms.'

All of the events I attended were question-answer sessions. These were at times moderated by someone and on other

occasions led to direct interactions with an audience. Being
with the audience directly was both challenging and enjoyable.
The tougher the audience, the more fun I had; it allowed me to
explore my creative side. There was a demand for my presence
in small and large gatherings. We moved around Delhi for a
while, then proceeded to Dehradun for the literature festival.
From Dehradun, we travelled to Ahmedabad and to Vadodara,
my birthplace.

Vadodara holds a special place in my heart; it brought back
floods of memories of Ba-Bapuji. Namaji and his father had
taken care of Ba-Bapuji. They had lived and worked with Ba-
Bapuji from a young age. Namaji is now sixty years of age and
Mahmad, his father had died at the age of ninety years. Namaji
had learned how to cook from Ba. When I called him to tell
him that I will visit him for lunch, he choked up and his voice
quivered. He prepared a fantastic feast for me and fifteen of
my fellow travellers. He remembered all my favourite foods and
cooked them with his wife and daughter-in-law. I felt Ba was
there in person, through Namaji, serving me. He would say,
'Ben this is also your favourite . . .' So pure, full of love, affection
and respect. I was in awe! I ate the delicacies with tears flowing
freely from my eyes, my mind full of beautiful memories of Ba-
Bapuji.

Before and after the meal, I spent precious moments with
Namaji, sitting on Bapuji's swing, resting against Bapuji's
pillows. I felt I was sitting with Ba-Bapuji on the swing and
reliving those moments. The tears broke the emotional bridge.
This very moment became filled with an unbreakable bond and
I will cherish it for eternity. Heike and Mirjam had never seen
me like this, crying like a child, tears rolling down my cheeks
uncontrollably. The sad part was that Ba-Bapuji were no longer
there and the beautiful farm where we lived was long gone.

The whole area is an ugly construction of cement and concrete, the small lake near our farm converted to a garbage dump. When I saw this, I was heartbroken and I have decided to create a project to clean up this area. Unfortunately, right now I am restricted due to the Coronavirus pandemic. I am eagerly waiting for the world to open up again so I can move on with this project.

From Vadodara, we went to Pune, which was originally not in our schedule, but the film crew suggested that I visit Pune.

It was a grey, rainy day when I reached Pune. The weather was a mirror of the sad end of Bhagwan and his life's work. I met Abhay Vaidya, the writer of the book *Who killed Osho?* He was knowledgeable, with information on Bhagwan after his return from the US and after I had left him. He told me how Bhagwan died and explained what he had written in his book.

I listened to his words with a heavy heart. Then Abhay took me to the crematorium where Bhagwan's body was cremated. I paid my respects to Bhagwan and bid him a final goodbye.

From Pune, we went to Mumbai. I had a talk in Soho house with some Bollywood celebrities. The next day I shot an advertisement for my upcoming film with Shakun Batra.

In the evening, I visited one of Anurag's projects in the Mumbai slums. I was deeply touched by the work Anurag and his project were doing for the slum dwellers.

I want to say a few words about Anurag. He is a young man of about twenty-five years, young but intelligent, sensitive and capable. It was his invitation that brought me to India after three-and-a-half decades. I thank him for the love and kindness he displayed towards me and wish him luck and success in the future. Bhagwan had often talked about the two certainties of life: change and death. He said that you cannot step twice in the same flowing water. Change is imminent. Death is the culmination of life. It is the highest point of life. No one can escape it. No one is spared from it.

If you understand it, you will not be afraid of change and death in life.

Bhagwan illustrated this through the story of a woman and her young son, who had passed away. The mother went to Buddha to bring the young son back to life. Buddha in turn sent the woman to bring some rice from a house where no one had died before. The woman runs through the village looking for a house where no one had died before. In the evening, she returns to Buddha disheartened. She hadn't found a house where someone had not died.

Buddha explained that death is the law of nature; one who is born will die. There are no exceptions. The story reminded me of the fear I felt when Chinmaya's death was hanging over our head from the time we had met each other. Chinmaya was diagnosed and treated for Hodgkin's, a cancer of the lymphatic system. He had been given a year and a half to two years to live in 1969. I had expressed my concern and worry about it to Bhagwan. Bhagwan did not comfort me with sympathetic words, but he walked me through my fear of death with logic.

He explained, 'Death is certain for Chinmaya just as it is for everyone who is ever born. Seela, you and Chinmaya have the good fortune of not ignoring death. Now that death is coming, welcome it. You should wait for it with open arms. Until it arrives you should enjoy each other and celebrate the life you have together. Don't waste it in ugly jealousy and possessiveness . . .'

Bhagwan's explanation of the concepts of change and death went right into our hearts. We started joking about death and living in the moment and suddenly the sorrow that hung over us started disappearing. Our days were busy with work and nights free of worry. We ended up spending a number of good years, in spite of Chinmaya's illness, together in Poona Ashram among Bhagwan and his sanyasins.

Each time Bhagwan spoke of death and dying, our understanding of the same deepened. For me, the key was the unfulfilled desires that made it difficult to digest death. Bhagwan's teaching of complete acceptance of life made it easier to let go.

When Chinmaya died, Bhagwan told me to go to sleep for three days and nights. When I woke up, he suggested I should distribute all his belongings among people who had helped him and were his friends. I should not hold on to anything except loving memories and bury myself in work. I followed Bhagwan's instructions completely. His wisdom and understanding of the death of a loved one made it easier for me to live through it. Since Chinmaya's death, I have lost a number of loved ones. I have followed the same process, the same guidance and wisdom shared with me by Bhagwan. And I can tell you that it works.Today, I live my life spreading Bhagwan's teachings. Perhaps many of his other followers are also doing the same. As long as I am alive, his work will continue to survive.

Bhagwan once told me a beautiful story.

A Samurai goes to a Zen Master to learn about the mysteries of life.

The Samurai asks respectfully: 'Master, please show me the gates of hell, so I can avoid them . . .'

The Master started insulting the Samurai with obscene words.

The Samurai was shocked by the Master's behaviour. Angry and full of rage from the insults, he pulls the sword out of its sheath.

Just then, the Master shouts: 'Here open the Gates of Hell!'

The Samurai, understanding fully, puts his sword back in the sheath.

The Master says with respect: 'Here open the Gates of Heaven!'

I am who I am, fully comfortable in my skin. That is what is important to me. I do not need anyone's approval of my character. Not from Bhagwan, his people or the media. The question is not how I deal with it, but how they live with it. Just to assassinate someone's character on hearsay without knowing the truth is unfair. As for me, I remain untouched by it. I have learned and I continue to learn every day of my life. I remain forever grateful to Existence.

List of Sources

'Oh No, It's Osho: A Villain Speaks from beyond the Grave.' *The Baltic Times.* Accessed 17 June 2020. https://www. baltictimes.com/news/articles/19770/.

Singh, Pooja. 'I Have Come out as a Winner: Ma Sheela Anand.' *Mint.* 29 September 2019. Accessed 1 June 2020. https:// www.livemint.com/news/india/-i-have-come-out-as-a- winner-11569774696045.html.

Sheela, Anand. *Dont Kill Him!: The Story of My Life with Bhagwan Rajneesh: A Memoir* (New Delhi: Finger Print, 2012).

Acknowledgements

I would like to take this opportunity to thank the Matrusaden and Bapusaden teams in Switzerland, Mauritius and Vietnam. Similarly, Anurag Chauhan and Humans for Humanity's support has been invaluable. Also, Meeta Gutgutia and Sukirti Gupta of Sipping Thoughts; Anurag Batra of Business World; Sanjay Garg of Raw Mango; and Sonal Mehta and friends.

YPO (Gujarat, Delhi and Pune), FICCI, CII, Zorba the Buddha—I am grateful for your love. I would also like to extend my gratitude to Karan Johar; Laxmi Narayan Tripathi and friends; Shakun Batra and his film crew; Bina Ramani; Disha Batra; and Namaji Mahmad Kureshi. And finally, Milee Ashwarya and the Penguin Random House India team.

There were many that have helped me—those directly or indirectly involved; many journalists and representatives of the media that will go unnamed. I thank you all.